The Imitation of Christ

With

Devotional & Study Guide

Thomas a Kempis

21st Century Version, Guide and Commentaries
by J.D. Nelson

Permissions

Efforts have been made to indicate required permissions or be within fair use guidelines for quotations. This adaptation, interpretation and translation, apart from original material by J.D. Nelson, arises from works in the public domain. If any appropriate acknowledgements have been omitted or rights overlooked, please notify writer and publisher so subsequent editions may be corrected.

Johansson Garcia Publishing
World Literature Division

I have tried at times to recreate events from my memory. Names, businesses, places, chronologies and identifying details have been changed to protect the privacy of individuals; and composites are used. Any resemblance to actual persons, living or dead, or actual events is purely coincidental.

Table of Contents

FOREWORD

Small and modest churches have exercised an extraordinary impact on my life. Most of the churches where my father was a pastor as I grew up were small. The formative nature of my experience within and through such churches has been profound and powerful. It seems as if I was able to know well and distinctively the individuals and families in those churches where the community was bounded and graspable. For many of those years our family went to church three times a week, and almost everything in our lives related to the church. People and events remain clear and poignant in my memory: good friends, girls I liked, the humor and personalities of certain adults; youth groups, pot lucks and retreats; the events and feel of the Christmas and Easter seasons.

The demographic of the churches I attended was middle and lower middle class. There were men and women who were teachers, trades people, fire and police personnel, small business owners. In a small church, people's hardships and imperfections were often apparent. There was support, a capacity for embracing and enfolding, to get through hard times: through job loss, loss of a home, family and marital conflict, illness and death. There were vulnerabilities revealed and addressed which went to the core of that which is grace and mercy. The provision and receipt of love and grace was often dramatic and touching. There was always spiritual support and prayer, almost always a willingness to provide time and labor, and frequently a willingness to provide monetary help, housing and assistance in finding employment.

I obtained my first real job through a friend in the church, as a laborer at a construction company during all my summers of college. Most of the time I ran a machine and bent rebar of different diameters into angles and various shapes for placement as supports in construction. My fellow workers were men in their 30s, 40s and 50s, with wives or divorced, with children. They were good guys. I listened closely to the stories they told of their lives, the demands of raising children, the scarcity of money, of conflicts with spouses and the joys of drinking beer with buddies or in the peace of watching television.

The permanent employees worked steadily, without any extraneous effort. I do not think any of them had gone far past high school, but they were all very competent at what they did, working the equipment and iron easily. They were remarkably quick in the arithmetic which was frequently necessary. I was reasonably good at my work in the yard, but there was a smoothness in their movement, a multiplicative factor in how well they worked in relation to me. Another summer worker and I were not as intuitive and natural. Things would happen.

Once, the two of us were moving a large load of iron off a tractor trailer and into the yard using the overhead crane. We hooked it up from the truck and slowly moved it up and off the trailer and across the yard. Somehow we got the overhead crane's control box which hung down on a cable caught under the load of metal as we let it down in a suitable place. We walked around the rebar for a few minutes, discussing possible strategies of how to get at the control box, but we could not figure a way. Without access to the controls we could not move the iron off the control box. We looked up finally, realizing we would have to ask for help, and saw Jack the foreman and Fred the head bender watching us with amusement. Jack shook his head, and Fred muttered something about 'college boys' before using another crane to haul the rebar off the control box.

My parents and the members of our congregations modeled Biblical values and taught me how to live, even as they made mistakes and committed sins. They taught me the importance of work and how to work. I learned to arrive early at my place of employment, and to be reliable and constant in all matters. I learned to work hard, to the best of my abilities, with a positive attitude. I learned that my word should be my bond.

My parents and those churches provided a foundation for my character. They gave me a basic understanding of right and wrong. However, when I grew older, particularly after I entered the adult world, I found I was not entirely prepared for what I came to face within complex human institutions such as universities, corporations and other organizations where money and power were critical aspects of nature and being.

I needed to know how to be morally, and how to be ethically. Matters and issues arose which were not always clear, which at times seemed to have shades of grey. I needed to learn how to exist with integrity within my character and personality and being. The thoughtfulness and teaching of *The Imitation of Christ* helped me greatly. It helped me to understand how to live day by day with a large part of myself intertwined with Jesus Christ and the persons of God. Most significantly, it was when I could be imbued with the Holy Spirit and thinking of the book that I could be transformed in how I perceived the world and conducted myself.

How should one think about and worship Jesus Christ?

How should one live life?

These were two questions that *The Imitation of Christ* helped me answer. Even though I realized that part of the purpose of the book was to provide guidance for those in religious orders, it nevertheless had an enormous relevance for me and my life. It laid out for me in a direct and understandable way how to think about Jesus Christ, and how to live life as Christ would live it—with guidance and an integrity which was explicit and practical. The book has a distinctive intelligence, clear sightedness and wisdom.

Imitation developed and depicted Christ and His person and being in a startling and breathtaking manner, in a way I had never before seen. The worshipful and loving portrayal of Christ's beauty and character was a revelation. The book showed me how to better see and worship Jesus Christ. "My God, my love, You are all mine and I am all yours…You are my glory and the exultation of my heart." It also described, realistically and honestly, elements of the Christ-like life, the remarkable but challenging way of the cross and cost of discipleship. *Imitation* taught and created an appropriate mindset to make right decisions by emulating Christ through the power of the Holy Spirit. It caused me to understand that it is through the imitation of Jesus Christ within the power of the Holy Spirit that I can live the life God planned and dreamed for me.

INTRODUCTION

The *Imitation of Christ* was written and initially published anonymously in the early 15th Century, around 1418 to 1427. Thomas a Kempis is generally thought to be the author. Thomas was born about 1380 in Kempen, Germany, within the Lower Rhine region. He followed his older brother and went to a well respected school as an adolescent in Deventer, which is in the Netherlands. There, Thomas was exposed to the Brethren of the Common Life, a Roman Catholic movement which emphasized individual piety, an active and simple Christly life, and union with God.

This group arose in the context of the Devotia Moderna movement, a reform movement seeking to promote the vitality and practices of the first Christians and the early church. It was a response to the perception that there had been a deterioration of moral values among the clergy, priests and monks, and a deterioration in the rigor of their clerical and monastic practices, with resulting negative implications for the lay members of their congregations and communities. Over the course of time, this type of Catholic reform thinking and practice of the simple life had an impact on the Protestant Reformation occurring during the 16th century. Martin Luther and his Ninety Five Theses could be seen as an early point in 1517.

After finishing school, Thomas again followed his brother who had become prior or leader at the monastery of Mount St. Agnes in Zwolle, Netherlands. Thomas became a canon regular or priest. In addition to leading Mass and hearing confessions, he spent a great deal of time throughout the years as a copyist and writer. He is thought to have completely copied the Bible at least five times, and his writings utilize the scriptures constantly. One can frequently sense the voice and soul of the Bible in the *Imitation*. He became a sub-prior or leader within the monastery of Mount St. Agnes, and in that role was responsible for instructing and educating novices. He wrote booklets for that purpose with which the content and message of *Imitation* fit well. Thomas died in 1471.

Although not quite as well known by the common reader or Protestants in the present day, *Imitation* has historically been the most widely translated and read devotional and Christian classic after the Bible itself. The *Imitation* was organized in four books of varying length: 1) Thoughts Helpful in the Life of the Soul; 2) The Interior Life; 3) Internal Consolation; and 4) Invitation to Holy Communion. The books are reflective and thoughtful, while at the same time practical in identifying specific spiritual guidelines. In this version which I refer to as the 21st Century Version, I include all the chapters of the original for Books 1 and 2, but make particular critical selections for Books 3 and 4. For all four books I work to modernize principles and titles.

Approach

I wanted to make *The Imitation of Christ* easier to read and understand, and accessible to a wider readership for the 21st Century. My experience was that many individuals (including myself) bogged down in the middle of the book. Consequently, I wanted to create a version which highlighted critical passages, and moved the reader through the greater book efficiently. I also wanted to actively engage with the text and weave it into my being in a different way from the passive reading I had done for many years. Working on the selections and text of this version has allowed me to do that. This approach necessarily utilizes my sensibilities, and any and all shortcomings are consequently mine.

75 DAY DEVOTIONAL AND STUDY GUIDE

Please read the foreword and introduction prior to beginning the devotional and study guide. Within the guide, below, I provide questions for each chapter which should be useful for guiding thought and discussion.

Techniques and Strategies

I have found it beneficial to go over this book and material periodically and repeatedly in my life. It has been useful to do so as a devotional, and in shorter, more graspable segments. These methods have also helped me to integrate the book into my life, and make its thought and principles a part of my being. I have provided a devotional and study guide below with questions and concepts to review and consider.

It has been helpful to go through this material with a partner or a small group. That approach can help the book be more meaningful, vital and pleasant to review. More and greater insights can be gleaned with thoughtful discussion. It can be useful to have fellowship, shared energy and commitment, as well as accountability, for pursuing the imitation of Christ within oneself and one's community.

Daily Schedule Example For Working On Imitating Christ

Daily personal devotions
Family/Individual morning prayers
Mid-morning prayer and meditation
Lunchtime prayer and meditation

Mid-afternoon prayer and meditation
Dinner with family/self in God's presence
Family/Individual devotions and prayers

Weekly Goal: Work on one specific principle or concept for applying *The Imitation of Christ* within oneself for a week. Choose a new principle or concept each week for 10 weeks (70 days).

Start with what time you can responsibly devote, and you will often find you have more time than you realize. I find myself becoming more peaceful and productive within my spiritual life, and my working and family lives when I am able to pursue a schedule like the one above in a disciplined manner. Even two or a few minutes for many of the entries above can have a remarkable effect.

Devotional Guide and Study Questions

I) Book One: Thoughts Helpful in the Life of the Soul

1. Day 1, Ch. 1: Imitate Christ and Despise Empty Things of the World
    a) What should our chief effort as Christians be?
    b) What is vanity?
2. Day 2, Ch. 2: Fear God and Be Humble
    a) What should our approach be to knowledge?
3. Day 3, Ch. 3: Truth and Knowledge are in God

a) What makes up a "humble knowledge of self"?
b) What does it provide?

4. Day 4, Ch. 4: Be Careful and Patient
   a) How should we think and act?
5. Day 5, Ch. 5: Read the Bible with Humility and Faith
   a) How should we read Scripture?
   b) What do we gain?
6. Day 6, Ch. 6: Resist Carnal Passions
   a) How do you find peace of heart?
7. Day 7, Ch. 7: Trust in God, Not Yourself and Pride
   a) How should we think and act about ourselves?
8. Day 8, Ch. 8: How to be with Others
   a) How should we be with others?
9. Day 9, Ch. 9: Live with Obedience and Love
   a) What should our attitude be toward God?
10. Day 10, Ch. 10: Avoid Idle Talk
    a) How should we converse?
11. Day 11, Ch. 11: How to Find Peace
    a) What are ways in which to obtain peace?
12. Day 12, Ch. 12: The Value of Hardship
    a) What are benefits of adversity?
13. Day 13, Ch. 13: How to Resist Temptation
    a) What are elements of resisting temptation?
14. Day 14, Ch. 14: Avoid Rash Judgment
    a) How do you avoid rash judgment?

15. Day 15, Ch. 15: Do Work in Love and Charity
    a) How do you do works in love and charity?
16. Day 16, Ch. 16: Bear with the Faults of Others
    a) What are specific ways of bearing with others?
17. Day 17, Ch. 17: How to Live
    a) What are ways to live in peace with others?
18. Day 18, Ch. 18: Examples Set By Prior Followers of Christ
    a) What are elements of examples set for us by prior followers of Christ?
19. Day 19, Ch. 19: Practices of a Follower of Christ
    a) What are practices of a follower of Christ?
20. Day 20, Ch. 20: Love of Solitude and Silence
    a) How can you love solitude and silence?
21. Day 21, Ch. 21: Sorrow of Heart
    a) What are benefits of sorrow?
22. Day 22, Ch. 22: Thoughts on the Misery of Man
    a) What are benefits and implications of misery?
23. Day 23, Ch. 23: Thoughts on Death
    a) What are benefits of thinking of death?
24. Day 24, Ch. 24: God's Judgment and the Punishment of Sin

a) How can you prepare for the day of judgment?

25. Day 25, Ch. 25: Work Hard to Change Our Lives
    a) What are ways you can change to live well for God?

II) Book Two: The Interior Life

1. Day 26, Ch. 1: Meditation
    a) When can you meditate on God daily?
2. Day 27, Ch. 2: Humility
    a) How can you humble yourself regularly?
3. Day 28, Ch. 3: Peace and Goodness
    a) What are ways you can cultivate peace within yourself?
4. Day 29, Ch. 4: Simplicity and Purity
    a) What are ways you can cultivate purity within yourself?
5. Day 30, Ch. 5: How to Deal With Our Selves
    a) How should you approach your self?
6. Day 31, Ch. 6: The Joy of a Good Conscience
    a) What are consequences of a good conscience, as well as its absence?
7. Day 32, Ch. 7: Love Jesus Above All
    a) How can you love Jesus?
8. Day 33, Ch. 8: Intimacy with Jesus
    a) How can you be intimate with Jesus?
9. Day 34, Ch. 9: How to Approach Comfort

    a) What can you do when grace and comfort seem taken away?
10. Day 35, Ch. 10: Appreciate God's Grace
    a) What should your attitude be toward grace?
11. Day 36, Ch. 11: Few Truly Love the Cross of Jesus
    a) What are important aspects of suffering and the cross?
12. Day 37, Ch. 12: The Way of the Cross
    a) What does it mean to take up Jesus' cross?

III) Book Three: Internal Consolation (Particular Selections)

1. Day 38, Ch. 1: Conversation of Christ with the Faithful Soul
    a) What are various characteristics of those who are blessed?
2. Day 39, Ch. 4: Walk Before God in Humility and Truth
    a) What are truths to keep in mind as we walk with God?
3. Day 40, Ch. 5: The Wonderful Effect of God's Love
    a) What are aspects and effects of God's Love?
4. Day 41, Ch. 14: Consider God's Majesty and do not Become Proud
    a) What are aspects and implications of God's Majesty?

5. Day 42, Ch. 15: How One Should Speak and Feel
    a) How should one speak and feel?
6. Day 43, Ch. 16: True Comfort is Found in God Alone
    a) What are characteristics of the consolation found in God?
7. Day 44, Ch. 17: Place All Cares in God
    a) What attitudes should you have as you place your cares in God?
8. Day 45, Ch. 21: Rest in God
    a) What are interrelationships of worship and resting in God?
9. Day 46, Ch. 23: Four Principles Which Bring Great Peace
    a) What are the four principles which bring great peace?
10. Day 47, Ch. 24: Avoid Inappropriate Curiosity About Others' Lives
    a) What attitudes should you have about others' lives and why?
11. Day 48, Ch. 26: Obtain Freedom Through Prayer
    a) What are aspects of life which imprison us, and how can we be free?
12. Day 49, Ch. 27: Love of Self Greatest Obstacle in Life
    a) What elements of loving the self are challenges for you?
13. Day 50, Ch. 32: Pursue Self Denial and Renunciation

    a) How can you pursue self denial and renunciation?
14. Day 51, Ch. 33: Focus on Christ
    a) What are ways you can focus on Christ?
15. Day 52, Ch. 35: No Safety From Temptation; Seek God
    a) What are hardships you are likely to face, and how can you overcome them?
16. Day 53, Ch. 36: How to Approach The Judgment of Man
    a) What should your attitude be toward men and their judgments?
17. Day 54, Ch. 37: Renounce the Self to Obtain Freedom
    a) How can you renounce the self?
18. Day 55, Ch. 43: Beware Worldly Knowledge
    a) What are reasons to be wary of worldly knowledge?
19. Day 56, Ch. 46: Trust in God; Do Not Desire to Please Men
    a) What are benefits of trusting God and not pleasing men?
20. Day 57, Ch. 47: Work Faithfully and Bear Hardship for Eternity
    a) What are characteristics of eternity described in the passage?
21. Day 58, Ch. 48: Christ and Eternity will Overcome Sin and Evil
    a) What does the Disciple suffer from, and what does he seek?

22. Day 59, Ch. 53: God's Grace is Not Given to the Worldly Minded
    a) How does the voice of Christ advise the Disciple to be?
23. Day 60, Ch. 54: Nature Versus Grace
    a) What seems particularly true about your human nature from this passage?
24. Day 61, Ch. 55: The Corruption of Nature and Power of Grace
    a) What are a few beauties of God's grace?
25. Day 62, Ch. 56: Deny the Self and Imitate Christ, Bearing His Cross
    a) What are three key messages from this critical passage?
26. Day 63, Ch. 57: Do Not be Sad or Anxious
    a) What are ways to not be sad or anxious?
27. Day 64, Ch. 58: God Is Inscrutable
    a) What are aspects of God which make Him inscrutable?
28. Day 65, Ch. 59: Hope and Trust in God Alone
    a) What should our attitude be in placing our hope and trust in God?

IV) Book Four: Invitation to Holy Communion (Particular Selections)

1. Day 66, Ch. 1: Receive Christ with Reverence
    a) What occurs with and what results from the sacrament of communion?

2. Day 67, Ch. 2: God's Goodness and Love Are in the Sacrament of Communion
    a) What are attitudes the Disciple displays in relation to communion?
3. Day 68, Ch. 17: Receive Christ with Love and Desire
    a) What are aspects of the love and desire with which we should receive Christ?
4. Day 69, Ch. 18: The Importance of Faith
    a) What are elements of the importance of faith?
5. Day 70: Identify and review two favorite parts of Book One
6. Day 71: Identify and review two favorite parts of Book Two
7. Day 72: Identify and review two favorite parts of Book Three
8. Day 73: Identify and review two favorite parts of Book Four
9. Day 74: Summarize two lessons or truths that meant the most to you out of all the books, and explain why.
10. Day 75: Summarize two more lessons or truths out of all the books that meant the most to you, and explain why.

BOOK ONE: THOUGHTS HELPFUL IN THE LIFE OF THE SOUL

Chapter 1: Imitate Christ and Despise Empty Things of the World

"He who follows Me, walks not in darkness," says the Lord (John 8:12). By these words of Christ we are advised to imitate His life and habits if we wish to be enlightened and free from blindness of heart. Let our main effort be to study the life of Jesus Christ.

The teaching of Christ is better than the advice of saints, and he who has His spirit will find nourishment. There are many who hear the Gospel but do not care for it because they do not have the spirit of Christ. Whoever wishes to fully understand Christ's words must try to pattern his life on Christ.

What good does it do to speak learnedly about the Trinity if, lacking humility, you displease the Trinity? It is not learning that makes a man holy and just, but a virtuous life which makes him pleasing to God. I would rather feel contrition than know how to define it. What would it profit us to know the Bible by heart and the principles of philosophers if we live without grace and the love of God? All is vanity except to love God and serve Him.

The greatest wisdom is to seek the kingdom of heaven through contempt of the world. It is vanity to seek and trust in riches that perish. It is vanity to seek honor and be puffed with pride. It is vanity to follow the lusts of the body and desire things for which punishment will come. It is vanity to wish for long life and care little about a well-spent life. It is vanity to be concerned with the present and not make provision for things to come. It is vanity to love what is transient and not look ahead to where eternal joy abides.

Recall the proverb: "The eye is not satisfied with seeing nor the ear filled with hearing." [Eccles. 1:8] Try to turn your heart from a love of things visible toward that which is invisible. They who follow evil passions stain their conscience and lose the grace of God.

Chapter 2: Fear God and Be Humble

Man naturally desires knowledge [Aristotle, Metaphysics]; but what good is knowledge without the fear of God? Indeed a humble farmer who serves God is better than a proud intellectual who neglects his soul to study the course of the stars. [Augustine, Confessions V. 4] He who knows himself well becomes modest in his own eyes, and is not happy when praised by men.

If I knew all things in the world but do not have love, what will it profit me before God Who will judge me by my actions?

Avoid inordinate desire for knowledge which may bring anxiety, delusion and pride. Intellectuals like to seem learned and be called wise. Yet there is much knowledge which does little or no good for the soul. He who concerns himself excessively with things which do not relate to eternity is unwise.

Many words do not satisfy the soul; but a good life eases the mind and a clean conscience inspires trust in God. The more you know and the better you understand, the more severely will you be judged, unless your life is also more holy. Do not be proud because of your learning or skill. Have fear because of the talent given you. If you think you know many things and understand them, realize that there is much you do not know. Do not pretend wisdom, but admit your ignorance. Why prefer yourself to anyone else when many are more learned and more cultured than you?

If you wish to appreciate what is worthwhile, then desire to be unknown and considered as nothing. To know and despise one's self is the best and most perfect counsel. To think of oneself as nothing, and always think well and highly of others is the best and most perfect wisdom. If you see another sin or commit a crime, do not consider yourself better. You do not know how long you can remain blameless. All men are frail, and you must acknowledge that none are more frail than yourself.

Chapter 3: Truth and Knowledge are in God

Happy is he to whom truth shows itself, not in signs and words that fade, but as it actually is. Our opinions and senses often deceive us and we understand little.

What good is discussion of involved and obscure matters when our ignorance will not be held against us on Judgment Day? Neglect of things which are profitable and necessary, and excess concern for those which are irrelevant and harmful is folly.

We have eyes and do not see.

What have we to do with questions of philosophy? He to whom the Word of God speaks is free from speculating. From the Word are all things, and all things speak of God, Who also speaks to us. Without the Word no man understands or judges correctly. He to whom it becomes everything, who traces all things to it and who sees all things in it, may ease his heart and remain at peace with God.

O God, You Who are the truth, make me one with You in love. I am often wearied by many things I hear and read, but in You is all that I long for. Let the learned be still, let all creatures be silent before You. You alone speak to me.

The more at peace a man is, and the more simple of heart he becomes, the easier he understands sublime things. He can receive the light of knowledge from above. The pure, simple, and steadfast spirit is not distracted by multiple pursuits. He does all for the honor of God. He enjoys interior peace, and he seeks no selfish end in anything. What gives more trouble and affliction than uncontrolled desires of the heart?

A good and devout man arranges things he has to do not according to the whims of evil inclination, but according to right reason and conscience. Who struggles more than he who tries to master himself? This ought to be our purpose: to conquer the self, to become stronger each day, and be virtuous.

Every perfection in life has imperfection mixed in, and no learning is without darkness. Humble knowledge of self is a surer path to God than pursuit of learning. Not that learning is to be considered evil or knowledge which is good in itself. However, a clean conscience and virtuous life ought to be preferred. Many err and accomplish little because they try to become learned rather than live well.

If men used as much care in eliminating vice and cultivating virtue as they do in discussing problems, there would not be as much evil and scandal in the world or in religious organizations. On the day of judgment, we shall not be asked what we have read but what we have done; not how well we have spoken, but how well we have lived.

Tell me, where are all the teachers whom you knew well in life and who were famous for their learning? Others have already taken their places and I doubt they ever think of their predecessors. During life they seemed to be important; now they are hardly remembered. How quickly worldly glory passes away. If their lives had kept pace with their learning, then their study and reading would have been worthwhile.

How many perish because of selfish ambition and worldly knowledge and too little care for serving God. They became vain in their pride because they chose to be great rather than humble. He is great who has great love. He is great who is small in his own eyes and makes nothing of the highest honor. He is wise who looks upon earthly things as folly that he may gain Christ. He who does God's will and renounces his own is truly learned.

Chapter 4: Be Careful and Patient

Do not yield to impulse and suggestion but consider things carefully and patiently in the light of God's will. Very often we are so weak that we believe and speak evil of others rather than good. Good men do not believe every gossip, because they know that human frailty is prone to evil and appears in speech.

Do not act rashly or cling obstinately to your opinion. Do not believe everything people say or spread gossip you have heard.

Take counsel with a wise and conscientious man. Seek the advice of your betters in preference to following your own desires.

A good life makes a man wise according to God, and gives him broad experience. The more humble he is and more subject to God, the more wise and at peace he will be.

Chapter 5: Read the Bible with Humility and Faith

Truth, not eloquence, is to be sought in reading the Bible. Every part must be read in the spirit in which it was written. In the Scriptures we ought to seek profit rather than polished diction.

We ought to read simple and devout books as willingly as learned and profound ones. Do not to be swayed by the authority of the writer, whether he be a great literary light or an insignificant person, but by the love of simple truth. Do not ask who is speaking, but note what is said. Men pass away, but the truth of the Lord remains forever. God speaks to us in many ways without regard to persons.

Our anxieties impede our reading of the Bible. We worry over what we should read through the Holy Spirit.

If you would profit, read with humility, simplicity, and faith. Never seek a reputation for being learned. Listen attentively to the words of the saints. Do not be displeased with the sayings of the ancients, for they were not made without purpose.

Chapter 6: Resist Carnal Passions

When a man desires a thing too much, he becomes anxious. A proud and avaricious man never rests. He who is poor and humble of heart lives in a world of peace.

An undisciplined man is tempted and overcome in small evils. His spirit is weak, carnal and inclined to sensual things.

He can hardly abstain from earthly desires. It makes him sad to forego them. He is quick to anger if disciplined. Yet if he satisfies his desires, remorse overwhelms him because they did not lead to peace.

True peace is found in resisting passion, not satisfying them. There is no peace in the carnal man, but there is peace in the devout and spiritual man.

Chapter 7: Trust in God, Not Your Self and Pride

Vain is the man who puts his trust in men and created things.

Do not be ashamed to serve others for the love of Christ and seem poor in this world. Do not be self-sufficient, but place your trust in God. Do what lies in your power and God will aid your good will. Put no trust in your learning nor in the cunning of man, but rather in the grace of God who helps the humble and humbles the proud.

If you have wealth, do not glory in it, nor in friends who are powerful. Glory in God who gives all things and desires to give of Himself. Do not boast of your physical beauty, qualities which are marred by a little sickness. Do not take pride in your talents in case you displease God to whom belong your gifts.

Do not think yourself better than others in case you are considered worse before God who knows what is in man. Do not take pride in your deeds, for God's judgment differ from that of men and what pleases them often displeases Him. If there is good in you, see more good in others so that you may remain humble. It does no harm to think yourself less than others, but it is harmful to think yourself better than even one. The humble live in continuous peace, while in the hearts of the proud are envy and anger.

Chapter 8: How to Be With Others

Do not open your heart to every man, but discuss your affairs with those who are wise and fear God. Do not keep company with young people and strangers. Do not fawn upon the rich, and do not be fond of mingling with the great. Associate with the humble and the simple, with the devout and virtuous. Speak of edifying things. Do not be intimate with women, but commend all good women to God. Seek the intimacy of God and His angels, and avoid the notice of men.

We ought to love all men, but over familiarity with all is not good. Sometimes it happens that a person enjoys good reputation among those who do not know him, but is held in slight regard by those who do. We may think we are pleasing others by our presence, but may displease them through the faults they find in us.

Chapter 9: Live with Obedience and Love

It is a great thing to obey and not be one's own master, for it is safer to be subject than it is to command. Many live in obedience from necessity rather than love. They become discontented on slight pretext. They will never gain peace of mind unless they subject themselves wholeheartedly for the love of God.

Wherever you go, you will find no rest except in humble obedience to the rule of authority. Dreams of happiness through change or a change in place has deceived many.

Everyone wishes to do as he pleases and is attracted to those who agree with him. But if God be among us, we must at times give up our opinions for the blessings of peace.

Who is so wise that he can know everything? Do not trust excessively in your opinions, but be willing to listen to others. You will gain more merit if you accept another's opinion because of your love of God. It is often safer to listen to advice and take it than to give it. It may be that one's opinion may be good, but refusal to agree with others when reason demands it, is a sign of pride and obstinacy.

Chapter 10: Avoid Idle Talk

Avoid the gossip of men as much as possible, for discussion of worldly affairs, even though sincere, is a great distraction. We are quickly trapped and captivated by vanity.

Often I wish I had held my peace and had not spoken too much with others. Why do we converse and gossip among ourselves when we often come away with a troubled conscience? We do so because we seek pleasure and comfort from one another's conversation. We talk and think quite fondly of things we like very much or of things we dislike intensely. But, we often end by talking vainly and to no purpose. The external pleasure is an obstacle to inward and divine consolation.

We must watch and pray so time does not pass in idleness. When the right moment comes for speaking, say something edifying.

Bad habits and indifference to spiritual progress remove the guard from the tongue. Devout conversation is an aid to spiritual progress, especially when persons of the same mind and spirit associate together in God.

Chapter 11: How to Find Peace

We would have peace if we did not concern ourselves with what others say and do. These are not our concern. How can a man who meddles in others' affairs, seeks strange entertainments and is seldom tranquil, live long in peace?

Blessed are the simple of heart for they shall enjoy peace. Why were some saints given to contemplation? Because they worked to deny earthly desires within themselves, and to attach themselves to God with all their heart.

We are too occupied with our whims and fancies, too taken up with passing things. Rarely do we conquer even one vice. We are not driven by the desire to improve ourselves day by day. We remain cold and indifferent. If we controlled our bodies and allowed no distractions to enter our minds, we could appreciate the divine and experience heavenly contemplation.

The greatest obstacle is that we are not free from passions and lusts. We do not try to follow the way of Christ. When we encounter a difficulty, we are dejected and seek human comfort. If we tried to stand as brave men in battle, the Lord would sustain us. He Who gives us the opportunity to fight for victory, is ready to help those who trust in His grace.

If we let our religious life depend on the observance of externals, our devotion will come to an end. Let us be freed from our passions and thus have peace of mind.

If we were to uproot one vice each year, we should soon become perfect. The contrary is often the case. We feel we were better when we were first converted than after many years in the faith. Our progress ought to increase; yet it is considered noteworthy if a man can retain even a part of his initial fervor.

If we applied discipline at the start, we should be able to do all things with ease and joy. It is hard to break old habits, but harder still to go against our will.

If you do not overcome unimportant challenges, how will you overcome the more difficult? Resist temptation in the beginning, and eliminate the evil habit otherwise it may lead to more evil.

If you understood what peace a good life would bring to you and what joy it would give to others, you would be more concerned about your spiritual progress.

Chapter 12: The Value of Hardship

It is good for us to have trials for they remind us we are on probation and ought not hope in worldly things. It is good to suffer difficulty, to be misjudged by men even though we mean well. This helps us be humble and shields us from pride. When men do not think well of us, we are more inclined to seek God Who sees our hearts. A man should root himself in God so he will not need the comfort of men.

When a man of good will is tempted and tormented by evil thoughts, he realizes his greatest need is God. Without God he can do no good. Saddened by his miseries and sufferings, he laments and prays. He wearies of living and wishes for death so he may be with Christ. He understands perfect security and peace cannot be found on earth.

Chapter 13: How to Resist Temptation

As long as we live in this world we cannot escape suffering and temptation. It is written in Job: "The life of man upon earth is a warfare." [Job 7:1] Everyone must guard against temptation and must watch in prayer so the devil, who never sleeps but goes about seeking who he may devour, will not deceive him. No one is so perfect or holy that he is not tempted. Man cannot be free from temptation.

Temptations, though troublesome and severe, are often useful. In them, man is humbled, purified and instructed. Christ and saints passed through temptations and trials, and profited by them. Those who could not resist became corrupt and fell away. There is no state so holy, no place so secret that temptations and trials will not come. Man is never safe as long as he lives. They come from within us. We were born in sin. When one temptation passes, another comes. We shall always have something to suffer because we have lost our original blessedness.

Many people try to escape temptation, only to fall more deeply. We cannot conquer simply by fleeing, but through patience and humility we become stronger than our enemies. The man who avoids temptations outwardly and does not uproot them will make little progress. They will return more violent than before.

Little by little, with patience and longsuffering you will overcome, through God's help rather than austerity and your own rash ways. Take counsel when tempted. Do not be harsh with others who are tempted. Console them as you would wish to be consoled.

Temptation begins with a wavering mind and lack of trust in God. As a rudderless ship is driven here and there, so a careless man is tempted in many ways. Fire tempers iron and temptation steels the just. Often, we do not know what we can stand, but temptation shows us what we are.

Above all, we must be alert against the beginning of temptation, for the enemy is more easily conquered if he is refused admittance to the mind, and is stopped outside the door when he knocks.

Someone has aptly said: "Resist the beginnings; remedies come too late, when by long delay the evil has gained strength." First, a mere thought comes to mind, then strong imagination, followed by pleasure, evil delight and consent. Because he is not resisted in the beginning, Satan gains full entry. The longer a man delays in resisting, so much the weaker he become, while the strength of the enemy grows.

Some suffer great temptations at the beginning of their walk with God, others toward the end. Some are troubled almost constantly throughout their life. Others are tempted but lightly according to the wisdom and justice of God.

We should not despair when we are tempted, but pray to God that He may help us. According to Paul, He will not allow temptations that we cannot bear. Let us humble our souls in every trial and temptation for God will save and exalt the humble.

In temptations and trials the progress of a man is measured. In them, opportunity for merit and virtue is made manifest.

When a man is not troubled it is not hard for him to be fervent and devout. If he bears patiently in adversity, there is hope for great progress.

Some, guarded against great temptations, are overcome by small ones. Humbled by weakness in small trials, they may not presume on their own strength in great ones.

Chapter 14: Avoid Rash Judgment

Focus on yourself and beware of judging the actions of other men. In judging others a man labors vainly, often makes mistakes and easily sins. On the other hand, by judging and taking stock of himself he does something that is profitable.

We frequently judge things as we wish them to be. Through emotion true perspective is easily lost.

If God were the object of our desire, we should not be swayed easily by opposition to our opinions. But often something happens within or from without to draw us along.

Many seek themselves in things they do. They seem to enjoy peace of mind when things happen according to their wish and liking. If things happen other than they desire, they are disturbed and saddened. Differences of feeling and opinion often divide friends and acquaintances, even those who are religious and devout.

An old habit is hard to break, and no one is willing to be led farther than he can see.

If you rely upon your intelligence or industry rather than upon submission to Jesus Christ, you will have difficulty becoming an enlightened man. God wants us to be subject to Him, and through love, rise above human wisdom.

Chapter 15: Work in Love and Charity

Never do evil for anything in the world, or for the love of any man. For one who is in need, a good work may be left undone or changed for a better one. This is not omission of a good deed but rather its improvement.

Without love work is of no value, but anything done in love is fruitful. God weighs the love with which a man acts rather than the deed itself.

He does much who loves much. He does much who does a thing well. He does well who serves the common good rather than his own interests.

That which seems to be love is often sensuality, for man's inclination, his will, his hope of reward and self-interest are constant motives. He who has true and perfect love seeks himself in nothing, but seeks all for the glory of God. He envies no man, because he desires no personal pleasure nor does he wish to rejoice in himself. Rather, he desires the glory of God above all. He ascribes to man nothing that is good, but attributes it wholly to God from Whom all things proceed, and in Whom the blessed shall rest as their end and satisfaction.

If man had but a spark of love he would surely sense that all things of earth are full of vanity.

Chapter 16: Bear with the Faults of Others

Until God ordains otherwise, a man ought to bear patiently what he cannot correct in himself and in others. Consider it better to have your patience tested. Without patience and trial your merits are of little account. You should pray that God will help you bear them calmly.

If a person does not change, do not argue with him, but commit the matter to God so that His will and honor may be furthered. God knows how to turn evil to good. Try to bear with the defects and infirmities of others, because you also have faults others must endure.

If you cannot make yourself what you would like to be, how can you persuade others to your will? We want others to be perfect, yet we do not correct our own faults. We wish others to be corrected, yet we will not correct ourselves. Their freedom displeases us, yet we do not wish to be denied what we ask. We would have others bound by laws, yet we do not wish to be restrained. We seldom think of others as we do of ourselves.

If all were perfect, what should we have to suffer for God's sake? But God has ordained that we learn to bear with one another's burdens, for there is no man without fault, no man without burden, no man sufficient in himself or wise enough. We must support one another, console one another, mutually help and counsel. The measure of every man's virtue is best revealed in adversity; adversity that does not weaken a man but shows what he is.

Chapter 17: How to Live

If you wish peace with others, you must learn to compromise your will. To live in churches and communities, to remain without complaint and persevere faithfully is difficult. Blessed is he who lives a good life and ends his days in happiness.

If you would seek perfection, you must consider yourself a pilgrim, an exile on earth. If you would become a follower of Christ, you must be content to seem a fool for the sake of Christ. Habit and appearance change man little. It is a change in attitude and faith, the complete denial of self and desire that enables a true follower of Christ.

He who seeks anything other than God and the salvation of his soul will find trouble and grief. He who does not try to become the servant of all cannot remain at peace.

You have come to serve, not to rule. You must understand that you have been called to suffer and work. Do not idle and gossip away your time. Men are tried as gold in a furnace. No man can remain faithful unless he desires with his heart to humble himself before God.

Chapter 18: Examples Set By Prior Followers of Christ

Consider the examples of prior followers of Christ who possessed the light of true faith. What is our life compared with theirs? The saints and followers of Christ served the Lord in hunger and thirst, in cold and nakedness, in work and fatigue, in vigils and fasts, in prayers and meditation, in persecutions and afflictions. How many and severe were the trials they suffered--the apostles, martyrs, confessors, virgins, and all the rest who followed in Christ's footsteps. They denied their selves on earth so they might have life in eternity.

How strict and detached were the lives of the holy. What long and grave temptations they suffered. How often were they beset by the enemy. What frequent and ardent prayers they offered to God. What rigorous fasts they observed. How great their zeal and love for spiritual perfection. How brave the fight they waged to master their evil habits. What pure and straightforward purpose they showed toward God. By day they labored and by night they spent themselves in long prayers. Even at work they did not cease from mental prayer. They used all their time profitably. Every hour seemed too short for serving God. In the sweetness of contemplation, they forgot their bodily needs.

They renounced riches, dignities, honors and friends. They desired nothing of the world. They scarcely allowed themselves the necessities of life, and the service of the body. Even when necessary, it was irksome to them. They were poor in earthly things but rich in grace and virtue. Outwardly destitute, inwardly they were full of grace and divine comfort. Strangers to the world, they were close and intimate friends of God. To themselves they seemed as nothing, and they were despised by the world, but in the eyes of God they were precious and beloved. They lived in humility and obedience. They walked in love and patience, progressing on the path of spiritual life and obtaining favor with God.

They were examples for the faithful. Their power to stimulate us to perfection ought to be greater than of the lukewarm to tempt us to laxity.

How great was the fervor of the faithful at the beginning of their journey with Christ. How great their devotion in prayer and their pursuit of virtue. What splendid discipline flourished among them. What great reverence and obedience. The footsteps they left behind still bear witness that they were holy men who fought bravely to conquer the world.

Today, he who is not a transgressor and who can bear the duties which he has taken upon himself is considered great. How lukewarm and negligent we are.

We lose our original fervor quickly and become weary of life from laziness. You who have seen examples of the devout, do not fall asleep in pursuit of virtue.

Chapter 19: Practices of a Follower of Christ

The life of a follower of Christ ought to abound in every virtue so that he is internally what he appears to be. There ought to be more within than appears on the outside. He who sees within is God. We ought to reverence God wherever we are and walk pure as the angels in His sight.

Each day we ought to renew our resolution and have passion as though it were the first day of our faith. We ought to say: "Help me, O Lord God, in my resolution and in Your holy service. Grant me now to begin perfectly, for thus far I have done nothing."

As is our intention, so will be our progress. He who desires perfection must be diligent. If the strong-willed man fails frequently, what of the man who makes up his mind half-heartedly? Many are the ways of failing. Even a slight omission of faith means a loss of some kind.

Just men depend on the grace of God rather than on their wisdom. In Him they confide every undertaking, for man proposes but God disposes. God's way is not man's. If a spiritual practice is omitted out of piety or in the interests of another, it can be resumed later. But if it be abandoned carelessly, through weariness or neglect, then the fault may prove hurtful. Much as we try, we fail easily. We must have purpose, especially against things which besiege us. Our outward and inward lives must be closely watched and ordered, for both are important.

If you cannot compose yourself in Christ continuously, do so at least once a day in the morning or evening. In the morning make a resolution. In the evening examine yourself on what you have said, and what you have done and thought through the day. Consider whether you have offended God and those about you.

Arm yourself against the devil's assaults. Curb your appetite and you will curb inclinations of the flesh. Never be completely unoccupied, but read or write or pray or meditate or do something for the common good. Bodily discipline must be undertaken with discretion. It is not to be practiced indiscriminately by everyone.

Devotions not common to all are not to be displayed in public. Such personal things are better performed in private. Beware of indifference to community prayer through love of your own devotions.

Everyone need not have the same devotions. One suits this person, another that. Different practices are suitable for different times, some for holidays and some for weekdays. In time of temptation we need certain devotions. For days of rest and peace we need others. Some are suitable when we are sad, others when we are joyful in the Lord.

We ought to fix our purpose as though we were to pass from this world and come to eternity. We ought to prepare ourselves to live holy lives, as though we were soon to receive from God the reward of our labors. Let us realize we are not well prepared and that we are not worthy of the glory that shall in time be revealed to us. Let us try to prepare ourselves better for death.

“Blessed is the servant," says Christ, "whom his master, when he cometh, shall find watching. Amen I say to you: he shall make him ruler over all his goods." [Luke 12:43, 44]

Chapter 20: Love of Solitude and Silence

Seek a suitable time and meditate often on the favors of God. Leave unnecessary matters alone. Read that which bring sorrow to the heart rather than occupation to the mind. If you refrain from unnecessary talking and running about and from gossip, you will find enough time for holy meditation.

Many people of faith avoid company and chose to serve God in quiet. "As often as I have been among men," said one writer, "I have returned less a man." We often find this to be true when we take part in long conversations. It is easier to be silent than to not speak excessively. To stay at home is easier than to be on guard while away. Anyone who aims to live the spiritual life must be with Jesus, and apart from the crowd.

No man appears in safety before the public unless he first relishes obscurity. No man is safe in speaking unless he loves to be silent. No man rules safely unless he is willing to be ruled. No man commands safely unless he has learned well how to obey. No man rejoices safely unless he has within him a good conscience.

The security of followers of Christ was always found within the fear of God. They were not less cautious and humble when they were exercised virtue and grace. The security of the wicked, on the contrary, springs from pride and presumption, and will end in their own deception.

Never promise yourself security in life, even though you are a devout follower of Christ. Those whom men esteem highly are endangered by their own confidence. For many it is better to not be free from temptation, but to be tested so they do not become secure, filled with pride, or eager to fall back upon comfort.

If a man does not seek transient joys or worldly matters, he would have a good conscience. Peace and tranquility would be his, if he cut away anxiety and thought of divine and helpful things, and put his trust in God.

No man deserves the consolation of heaven unless he is contrite. If you desire sorrow of heart, seek privacy and shut out the uproar of the world. As it is written: "In your chamber bewail your sins." There you will find what you lose when in the world.

Your devotions will become dear to you if you exercise them, but if you do not, they will become wearisome. If, from the beginning of your faith, you live with your devotions, they will become a resource and comfort.

In silence and quiet the devout soul advances in virtue and learns the hidden truths of Scripture. There she finds a flood of tears with which to bathe and cleanse herself nightly. She can become intimate with her Creator the more she withdraws from the tumult of the world. God and His angels will draw near to him who withdraws from friends and acquaintances.

It is better for a man to be unknown and attend to his salvation than to neglect it and work miracles. It is praiseworthy for a monk to seldom leave his community, to flee the sight of men and have no wish to see them.

Why wish to see what you are not permitted to have? "The world passes away and the concupiscence thereof." Sensual craving sometimes entices you to wander, but when the moment is past, what do you bring back with you except a disturbed conscience and heavy heart? A happy going often leads to a sad return; a merry evening to a mournful dawn. Carnal joy begins sweetly but in the end brings remorse and death.

What can you find elsewhere that you cannot find in worshiping God? Behold heaven and earth and all the elements, of which all things are made. What can you see anywhere under the sun that will remain long? Perhaps you think you will satisfy yourself, but you cannot do so. If you should see all things, what would they be but an empty vision?

Raise your eyes to God and pray because of your sins and shortcomings. Leave vanity to the vain. Set yourself to that which God has commanded you to do. Close the door upon yourself and call to Jesus, your Beloved. Remain with Him in your thoughts, for nowhere else will you find peace. If you had not listened to gossip, you would have remained in peace. But since you love to hear news, it is only right that you should suffer sorrow from it.

Chapter 21: Sorrow of Heart

If you wish to make progress in virtue, live in the fear of the Lord. Do not look for excess freedom, discipline your senses, and shun silliness. Sorrow opens the door to many a blessing which dissoluteness usually destroys.

It is a wonder that any man who considers and meditates on his separation from God and the many dangers to his soul, can ever be perfectly happy in life. Lighthearted and heedless of our defects, we do not feel the real sorrows of our souls. We often indulge in empty laughter when we have good reason to weep. No liberty is true and no joy is genuine unless it is founded in the fear of the Lord and a good conscience.

Happy is the man who can throw off the weight of care and compose himself in contrition. Happy is the man who casts from him all that can burden his conscience.

Fight like a man. Habit is overcome by habit. If you leave men alone, they will leave you alone to do what you need do.

Do not busy yourself about the affairs of others and do not become entangled in the business of your superiors. Keep an eye on yourself and admonish yourself instead of your friends.

If you do not enjoy the favor of men, do not let it sadden you. Consider it a serious matter if you do not conduct yourself as carefully as is becoming for a servant of God.

It is safer to have few consolations in life, especially comforts of the body. If we do not have divine consolation or experience it rarely, it is our own fault because we do not seek sorrow and do not forsake vain satisfactions.

Consider yourself unworthy of solace and deserving rather of tribulation. When a man is perfectly contrite, the whole world is bitter and wearisome to him.

A good man finds enough over which to mourn. Whether he thinks of himself or his neighbor, he knows no one lives without suffering. The closer he examines himself the more he grieves.

The sins and vices in which we are entangled that distract us from contemplation of heaven are matters for sorrow and remorse.

I do not doubt that you would correct yourself if you would think more of an early death than a long life. If you thought in your heart of the future pain of hell, you would work hard and not fear hardship. Since these thoughts never touch the heart and since we are enamored of pleasure, we remain cold and indifferent. Our body complains easily because our soul is too lifeless.

Pray humbly to the Lord that He may give you a spirit of contrition. Say with the Prophet: "Feed me, Lord, with the bread of mourning and give me to drink of tears in full measure." [Ps. 80:9]

Chapter 22: Thoughts on the Misery of Man

Wherever you are or go, you are miserable unless you turn to God. Do not be dismayed when things do not happen as you wish and desire. Is there anyone who has everything as he wishes? No--neither I, nor you, nor anyone on earth. There is no one in the world who does not suffer trial and anguish.

Who is better off then? Surely, it is the man who will suffer something for God. Many unstable and weak-minded people say: "See how well that man lives, how rich, how great he is, how powerful and mighty." You must lift your eyes to the riches of heaven and realize that the material goods of which they speak are nothing. These things are uncertain and burdensome because they are not possessed without anxiety and fear. Happiness does not consist in the possession of abundant goods. A little is enough.

Living on earth is a misery. The more a man desires spiritual life, the more bitter the present becomes. He understands the defects and corruption of human nature. To eat and drink, to watch and sleep, to rest, to labor and be bound by other human necessities is certainly an affliction to the devout man. He would gladly be released from them and be free from sin. The inner man is burdened in this world by the necessities of the body, and for this reason the Prophet prayed that he might be as free from them as possible, when he said: "From my necessities, O Lord, deliver me." [Ps. 34:17]

Woe to those who do not know their misery, and greater woe to those who love this miserable and corruptible life. Some can scarcely obtain its necessities by work or begging. Yet they love it so much that if they could live here always, they would care nothing for the kingdom of God.

How foolish and faithless are those who are engrossed in earthly things so as to relish nothing but what is carnal. Miserable indeed, for in the end they will see to their sorrow how cheap and worthless was the thing they loved.

The saints of God and devout friends of Christ did not look to what pleases the body nor to the things that are popular. Their whole hope and goal centered on the eternal good. Their whole desire pointed to the lasting and invisible realm, so that love of what is earthly would not drag them down.

Do not lose heart in pursuing your spiritual life. There is time, and your hour is not past. Why delay your purpose? Begin at once and say: "Now is the time to act, now is the time to fight, now is the proper time to change."

When you are troubled and afflicted, that is the time to gain merit. You must pass through water and fire before coming to rest. Unless you deny yourself you will not overcome vice.

So long as we live in this fragile body, we can neither be free from sin nor live without weariness and sorrow. Gladly would we rest from misery, but in losing innocence through sin we also lost blessedness. We must have patience and await the mercy of God until iniquity passes, until mortality is swallowed up in life.

How great is the frailty of human nature which is prone to evil. Today you confess your sins and tomorrow you again commit the sins which you confessed. One moment you resolve to be careful, and after an hour you act as though you had made no resolution.

Because of our feebleness, we must humble ourselves and never think highly of ourselves. Through neglect we may lose what by grace we have acquired through long, hard labor. What will become of us who grow lukewarm? Woe to us if we presume to rest in peace and security when actually there is no holiness in our lives. It is beneficial for us to be instructed in the principles of good life, to gain hope of change and spiritual progress.

Chapter 23: Thoughts on Death

Your life on earth will end soon. Consider what may be in store for you. Today we live; tomorrow we die and are forgotten. Dull and hard is a heart which looks only to the present instead of preparing for what is to come.

In every deed and thought act as though you were to die this day. If you have a good conscience you would not fear death much. It is better to avoid sin than fear death. If you are not prepared today, how will you be prepared tomorrow? Tomorrow is uncertain. How do you know you will have a tomorrow?

What good is it to live a long life when we progress little in that life? Long life does not always benefit, but frequently adds to our guilt. Would that we lived well through one day. Many count up the years they have spent in faith, but find their lives made little holier. If it is terrifying to die, it is possible that to live longer is more dangerous. Blessed is he who keeps death before his eyes and prepares for it daily.

If you have seen a man die, remember that you must go the same way. In the morning consider that you may not live till evening. When evening comes do not dare to promise yourself the dawn. Be ready, and live so that death will never take you unprepared. Many die suddenly and unexpectedly, and in an unexpected hour the Son of God will come. When that last moment arrives you will have a different opinion of the life that has passed, and you will regret that you were careless and remiss.

How happy and prudent is he who tries in life to be what he wants to be in death. Contempt of the world, a desire to advance in virtue, a love for discipline, readiness to obey, self-denial, and endurance of hardship for the love of Christ will give a man expectations of a happy death.

You can do good works in good health. What can you do when you are ill? Few are made better by sickness. Likewise they who undertake many pilgrimages seldom become holy.

Do not put your trust in friends and relatives, and do not put off care of your soul till later. Men will forget you more quickly than you think. It is better to send a good account ahead of you than to rely on the help of others. If you do not care for your welfare now, who will care when you are gone?

The present is precious. These are days of salvation. Now is the acceptable time. How sad that you do not spend time in which you might purchase everlasting life in a better way. The time will come when you will want just one day, just one hour in which to make amends. Who knows whether you will obtain it?

See the danger from which you can free yourself and the fear from which you can be saved. Be wary and mindful of death. Try to live now in such a manner that at the moment of death you may be glad rather than fearful. Learn to die to the world now, so that you may begin to live with Christ. Learn to spurn all now, so you may freely go to Him. Chastise your body now, so you may have confidence.

Ah, foolish man, why do you plan to live long when you are not sure of living even a day? How many have been deceived and suddenly snatched away! How often have you heard of persons killed by drowning, fatal falls from high places, at meals or play, in fires, by the sword, in pestilence, or at the hands of robbers. Death is the end of everyone and the life of man passes quickly like a shadow.

Who will remember you when you are dead? Who will pray for you? Do what you can now, because you do not know when you will die, nor what your fate will be after death. Gather for yourself the riches of eternity while you have time. Think of nothing but your salvation. Care only for things of God. Honor Christ, imitate His actions, so that when you depart this life He will receive you.

Keep yourself as a stranger on earth. Keep your heart free and raise it to God. You do not have a lasting home here. Direct your prayers to Him, your sighs and tears, so that your soul may pass in happiness to the Lord after death.

Chapter 24: God's Judgment and the Punishment of Sin

In all things consider the end. How will you stand before the Judge from whom nothing is hidden and who will pronounce judgment with justice, accepting neither bribes nor excuses. You, miserable and wretched sinner, who fear even the countenance of an angry man, what answer will you make to the God who knows all your sins? Why do you not provide for yourself against the day of judgment when no man can be excused or defended by another because each will have to answer for himself? In this life, your work is profitable, your tears acceptable, your sighs audible, your sorrow satisfying and purifying.

The patient man goes through a helpful purgatory when he grieves more for one who harms him than for his own injury; when he prays for his enemies and forgives offenses; when he does not hesitate to ask forgiveness of others; when he is more easily moved to pity than to anger; when he tries to bring the body into complete subjection to the spirit.

It is better to atone for sin now and to cut away vices than to keep them for purgation in the hereafter. We deceive ourselves by our love of the flesh. What will that fire feed upon but our sins? The more we spare ourselves now and the more we satisfy the flesh, the harder will be the judgment and the more of our life which will be burned.

A man will be punished for those things in which he has sinned. The lazy will be driven with burning prongs, and gluttons tormented with unspeakable hunger and thirst. The wanton and lust-loving will be bathed in burning pitch and foul brimstone. The envious will howl in their grief like mad dogs.

Every vice will have its proper punishment. The proud will be faced with confusion and the avaricious pinched with abject want. One hour of suffering will be more bitter than a hundred years of penance here. In this life, men sometimes rest from work and enjoy the comfort of friends, but the damned have no rest or consolation.

You must take care and repent of your sins now so that on the day of judgment you may rest secure with the blessed. On that day the just will stand firm against those who tortured and oppressed them. He who now submits humbly to the judgment of men will arise to pass judgment upon them. The poor and humble will have great confidence, while the proud will be struck with fear. He who learned to be a fool in this world and to be scorned for Christ will then appcar to have been wise.

In that day, every trial borne in patience will be pleasing and the voice of iniquity will be stilled. The devout will be glad. The irreligious will mourn. The selfless body will rejoice more than if it had been pampered with every pleasure. The cheap garment will shine with splendor and the rich one become faded and worn. The poor cottage will be more praised than the gilded palace. In that day patience will count more than all the power in this world. Obedience will be exalted above cleverness. A good conscience will gladden the heart of man more than the philosophy of the learned. Contempt for riches will be of more weight than every treasure on earth.

You will find more consolation in having prayed devoutly than in having eaten daintily. You will be happy that you preferred silence to gossip.

Holy works will be of greater value than pleasing words. Discipline in life will be more satisfying than earthly delights.

Learn to suffer little things now that you may not have to suffer greater ones in eternity. Prove here what you can bear. If you can suffer only a little now, how will you be able to endure eternal torment? If a little suffering makes you impatient now, what will hell fire do? You cannot have two joys. You cannot taste the pleasures of this world and afterward reign with Christ.

If your life to this moment had been full of honors and pleasures, what good would it do if at this moment you should die? All is vanity except to love God and to serve Him alone.

He who loves God with all his heart does not fear death or punishment or judgment or hell. Perfect love assures access to God.

It is no wonder that he who delights in sin fears death and judgment.

It is good that even if love does not restrain you from evil, at least the fear of hell does. The man who casts aside a fear of God cannot continue in goodness, but will fall into the traps of the devil.

Chapter 25: Work Hard to Change our Lives

Be watchful and diligent in God's service. Think of how you can be apart from the world. How can you live for God and become a spiritual man? Strive earnestly for perfection. In a short time you will receive the reward of your labor, and neither fear nor sorrow shall come to you at the hour of death.

Labor a little now, and you will find great rest and eternal joy. If you are faithful and diligent, God will be faithful and generous to reward. Continue to have hope of salvation, but do not act with pride or laziness.

One day when a man who wavered between hope and fear was struck with sadness, he knelt in prayer before the altar of a church. While meditating, he said: "Oh if I but knew whether I should persevere to the end!" Instantly he heard within the divine answer: "If you knew this, what would you do? Do now what you would do then and you will be quite secure." Immediately consoled and comforted, he resigned himself to the divine will and the uncertainty ceased. His curiosity no longer sought to know what the future held for him. He tried instead to find the perfect and acceptable will of God in every good work.

"Trust thou in the Lord and do good," says the Prophet; "dwell in the land and thou shalt feed on its riches." [Ps. 37:3]

There is one thing that keeps many from improving their lives—which is dread of the difficulty of battle. Certainly they who try to overcome obstacles outstrip others in the pursuit of virtue. A man makes the most progress and gains the most grace in those matters where he obtains victory over self and his will. Everyone has difficulties to meet and conquer. A diligent and sincere man will make great progress even though he has more passions than one who is even-tempered but less concerned about virtue.

Two things help advancement: to withdraw from vices to which nature is inclined, and to work for those graces which are most needed.

Study to guard against faults which displease you in others. Make the best of every opportunity. If you see good examples, imitate them. Take care so you are not guilty of that which you consider reprehensible. If you have been guilty of them, try to correct yourself as soon as possible. As you see others, so they see you.

How pleasant and sweet to behold brothers and sisters fervent and devout, well mannered and disciplined. How sad and painful to see them wandering, and not practicing the things to which they are called. How hurtful it is to neglect their calling and to attend to what is not their business.

Remember the purpose you have undertaken, and keep in mind the image of Jesus. Even though you may have walked for many years on God's path, you may become ashamed if you do not try to make yourself more like Him.

The Christian who concerns himself with our Lord's holy life and passion will find there an abundance of useful and necessary things. He need not seek for anything better than Jesus. If Christ should come to our hearts, how quickly and well we would learn.

A fervent Christian accepts all things commanded him and does them well. A negligent and lukewarm Christian has trial after trial. He suffers anguish because he has no comfort within and cannot find it without. The Christian who does not live up to his faith exposes himself to ruin. He who wishes to be unrestrained will always be in trouble, for something will always displease him.

Think of those who live a contemplative life, whose food is poor, who work hard, and spcak but little, rise early and pray much, read frequently and subject themselves to discipline. Think of those who rise to sing praises to the Lord. Do not grow lazy in your faith when so many Christians have begun to rejoice in God's power.

If there were nothing else to do but praise the Lord with all your heart and voice. If you had never to eat, or drink or sleep, but could praise God and occupy yourself with spiritual pursuits, how much happier you would be than you are now, a slave to every necessity of the body. Would that there were no such needs, but only the spiritual food of the soul which we taste so seldom.

When a man reaches a point where he seeks no comfort from anyone, he begins to relish God perfectly. Then he will be content no matter what may happen to him. He will neither rejoice over great things nor grieve over small ones, but will place himself entirely in the hands of God, who for him is all in all.

Always remember your end and do not forget that lost time never returns. Without diligence you will never acquire virtue. When you begin to grow lukewarm, you are falling into the beginning of evil. If you give yourself to faith, you will find peace and experience less hardship because of God's grace and the love of virtue.

A fervent and diligent man is ready for all. It is greater work to resist vice and passion than to sweat in physical toil. He who does not overcome small faults, shall fall little by little into greater ones.

If you have spent the day profitably, you will always be happy in the night. Watch over yourself, warn yourself, and regardless of what becomes of others, do not neglect your faith. The more you deny your self, the more progress you will make.

BOOK TWO: THE INTERIOR LIFE

Chapter 1: Meditation

The kingdom of God is within you," says the Lord. [Luke 17:21]

Turn to God with all your heart. Forsake this wretched world and your soul shall find rest. Learn to despise the external, and devote yourself to what is within. You will see the kingdom of God come unto you, the kingdom which is peace and joy in the Holy Spirit.

Christ will come to you offering consolation if you prepare a dwelling for Him in your heart--whose beauty and glory He will take delight in. Christ visits and His communion is sweet and full of consolation. His peace is great, and His intimacy wonderful.

Faithful soul, prepare your heart for this Bridegroom that He may come and dwell within you. He Himself says: "If any one love Me, he will keep My word, and My Father will love him, and We will come to him, and will make Our abode with him." [John 14:23]

Give place to Christ, but deny entrance to others. When you have Christ you are rich and He is sufficient for you. He will provide for you. He will supply your every want, so that you need not trust in frail, changeable men. Christ remains forever, standing firmly with us to the end.

Do not place confidence in weak and mortal man, helpful and friendly though he be. Do not grieve if he opposes and contradicts you. Those who are with us today may be against us tomorrow, for men change with the wind. Place all your trust in God. Let Him be your fear and your love. He will answer for you. He will do what is best for you.

You have no lasting home on earth. You are a stranger and a pilgrim wherever you may be. You shall have no rest until you are united with Christ.

Why do you look about when the world is not the place of your rest? Dwell upon heaven and give only a glance to earthly things. They pass away, and you with them. Take care that you do not cling to them or you may be entrapped and perish. Fix your mind on the Most High, and pray unceasingly to Christ.

If you do not know how to meditate on heavenly things, direct your thoughts to Christ's crucifixion and behold His sacred wounds. If you turn to the sacrifice and grace of Christ, you will find comfort in suffering. You will not mind the scorn of men, and you will bear their slanderous talk.

When Christ was in the world, He was despised by men. In the hour of need He was forsaken by acquaintances and left by friends to the depths of scorn. He was willing to suffer and be despised. Do you dare to complain? He had enemies and defamers. Do you want everyone to be your friend, your benefactor? How can your patience be rewarded if no adversity tests it? How can you be a friend of Christ if you are not willing to suffer hardship? Suffer with Christ and for Christ if you wish to reign with Him.

If you once entered into communion with Jesus or tasted His love, you would care nothing for your comfort but would rejoice in the reproach you suffer. Love of Christ makes a man despise himself.

A man who is a lover of Jesus and truth, a man who is free from uncontrolled desires can turn to God and rise above himself to enjoy spiritual peace.

He who tastes life as it really is, not as men say or think, is wise with the wisdom of God rather than of men.

He who learns to live the spiritual life and to take little account of earthly things does not seek special places or times to practice their faith. A spiritual man composes himself because he has never wasted his attention upon externals. No outside work stands in his way. He adjusts himself to things as they happen. He whose disposition is ordered cares nothing about the perverse behavior of others. A man is upset and distracted only in proportion as he engrosses himself in earthly matters.

If you were purified from all sin and all was well with you, everything would be to your good and profit. Because you are neither dead to self nor free from earthly desire, there is much that displeases and disturbs you. Nothing defiles the heart of man as impure attachment to created things. If you refuse earthly consolation, you will be able to contemplate heavenly things and experience joy.

Chapter 2: Humility

Be not troubled about those who are with you or against you, but take care that God be with you in everything. Keep your conscience clear and God will protect you. The malice of man cannot harm someone God wishes to help. If you know how to suffer in silence, you will experience God's help. He knows when and how to deliver you. Place yourself in His hands, for it is His prerogative to help and free men from distress.

It is good to have others know and rebuke our faults, for it gives us humility. When a man humbles himself because of his faults, he appeases those who are angry with him.

It is the humble man whom God protects and liberates. It is the humble whom He loves and consoles. To the humble He turns and bestows great grace. After their humiliation He may raise them up to glory. He reveals His secrets to the humble, and with kindness bids them come to Him. The humble man enjoys peace in the midst of trouble, because his trust is in God not in the world. You must not think that you have made progress until you can look upon yourself as inferior to all others.

Chapter 3: Peace and Goodness

Keep peace with yourself; then you will be able to bring peace to others. A peaceful man does more good than a learned man. A man of passions turns even good to evil and is quick to believe evil. The peaceful man, being good himself, turns all things to good.

The man who is at ease is never suspicious, but the disturbed and discontented spirit is beset with suspicions. He neither rests nor permits others to do so. He often says what should not be said and does not do what ought to be done. He is concerned with the duties of others but neglects his own.

Direct your zeal first toward yourself. Then you may exercise it upon those around you. You are proficient at explaining your actions with excuses which you would not accept from others. It would be more just to accuse yourself and excuse your brother. If you wish men to be patient with you, you must be patient with them. How far you are from love and humility which does not know how to be angry with others, or be indignant only against yourself.

It is no great thing to associate with the good and gentle, for that is pleasing. Everyone enjoys a peaceful life and prefers congenial persons. To be able to live at peace with harsh and perverse men, or with the undisciplined and those who irritate us, is a grace, a praiseworthy and manly thing.

Some people live at peace with themselves and with their fellow men, but others are never at peace with themselves nor do they bring it to anyone else. These latter are a burden to everyone, but they are more of a burden to themselves. A few live at peace with themselves and try to restore it to others.

All our peace in this life is found in humbly enduring suffering rather than being free from it. He who knows how to suffer will enjoy peace, because he is the conqueror of himself, the master of the world, a friend of Christ, and an heir of heaven.

Chapter 4: Simplicity and Purity

A man is raised from the earth by two wings--simplicity and purity. There must be simplicity in his intention and purity in his desires. Simplicity leads to God, and purity embraces and enjoys Him.

If your heart is free from inappropriate desires, no good deed will be difficult for you. If you seek nothing but the pleasure of God and the welfare of your neighbor, you will enjoy freedom.

If your heart is right, everything will be a mirror of life for you and a book of holy teaching. There is no creature so small and worthless that it does not show the goodness of God. If you are good and pure, you will see all things clearly and understand them. A pure heart penetrates to heaven and hell. As a man is within, so he judges what is without. If there is joy in the world, the pure of heart possess it. If there be anguish and affliction, an evil conscience knows it well.

As iron cast into fire loses its rust and becomes glowing white, so he who turns to God will be stripped of laziness and changed into a new man. When a man begins to grow lax, he fears work and welcomes comfort. When he begins to conquer himself and walk bravely in the ways of God, then he thinks less difficult what he thought hard before.

Chapter 5: How to Deal With Our Selves

We must not rely too much upon ourselves, for grace and understanding are often lacking in us. We have but little inborn light, and this we quickly lose through negligence. Often we are not aware that we are blind. Meanwhile we do wrong, and then do worse in excusing it. At times we are moved by passion, and we think it zeal. We take others to task for small mistakes, and overlook greater ones in ourselves. We are quick to brood over things we suffer from others, but think nothing of how much others suffer from us. If a man would weigh his deeds fully and rightly, he would find little cause to pass judgment on others.

The inward man puts the care of his soul before other concerns. He who attends to himself carefully does not find it hard to hold his tongue about others. You will never be devout unless you are silent about others and pay particular attention to yourself. If you attend to God and yourself, you will not be disturbed by what you see around you.

Where are your thoughts when they are not upon your soul? What have you gained if you have neglected your soul? If you wish to have peace of mind and unity of purpose, you must cast all else aside and keep your soul before your eyes.

You will make great progress if you keep your soul free from temporal cares, for to value anything that is temporal is a mistake. Consider nothing great, nothing high, nothing pleasing, nothing acceptable, except God or that which is of God. Consider the consolations of creatures as vanity, for the soul that loves God scorns all things that are inferior to Him. God alone, the eternal and infinite, satisfies all, bringing comfort to the soul and true joy to the body.

Chapter 6: The Joy of a Good Conscience

The glory of a good man is the testimony of a good conscience. Keep your conscience good and you will enjoy happiness. A good conscience can bear a great deal and can bring joy in the midst of adversity. An evil conscience is ever restive and fearful. Sweet shall be your rest if your heart does not reproach you.

Do not rejoice unless you have done well. Sinners never experience true joy or peace, for "there is no peace to the wicked," says the Lord. [Isa. 48:22] Even if they say: "We are at peace, no evil shall befall us and no one dares to hurt us," do not believe them. The wrath of God will arise quickly, and their deeds will be brought to nothing and their thoughts will perish.

To glory in adversity is not hard for the man who loves, for this is to glory in the cross of the Lord. But the glory given or received of men is short lived. The glory of the world is accompanied by sorrow. The glory of the good is in their conscience and not in the lips of men. The joy of the just is from God and in God, and their gladness is founded on truth.

The man who longs for eternal glory does not care for that of time. He who seeks passing fame or does not in his heart despise it, cares little for the glory of heaven.

He who minds neither praise nor blame possesses great peace. If his conscience is good, he will be content and at peace.

Praise adds nothing to your holiness, nor does blame take anything from it. You are what you are, and you cannot be better than you are in God's sight. If you consider what you are within, you will not care what men say about you. They look to appearances but God looks to the heart. They consider the deed but God weighs the motive.

It is characteristic of a humble soul always to do good and to think little of itself. It is a mark of purity and faith to look for no consolation in created things. The man who desires no justification from without has clearly entrusted himself to God: "For not he who commendeth himself is approved," says St. Paul, "but he whom God commendeth." [2 Cor. 10:18]

To walk with God, to be free from external affection; this is the state of the inward man.

Chapter 7: Love Jesus Above All

Blessed is he who appreciates what it is to love Jesus and who despises himself for the sake of Jesus. Give up all other love for His, since He wishes to be loved above all things.

Affection for creatures is deceitful and inconstant, but the love of Jesus is true and enduring. He who clings to a creature will fall, but he who gives himself to Jesus will be strengthened.

Love Him. Keep Him as a friend. He will not leave you as others do, or let you suffer lasting death. Sometime you will have to part with everything. Cling to Jesus in life and death. Trust yourself to the glory of Him who alone can help you when all others fail.

Your Beloved is such that He will not accept what belongs to another. He wants your heart for Himself, to be enthroned there as King in His own right. If you but knew how to free yourself from creatures, Jesus would gladly dwell within you.

You will find that nearly all the trust you place in men is a loss. Neither confide in nor depend upon a wind-shaken reed, for "all flesh is grass" [Isa. 15:6] and all its glory, like the flower of grass, will fade away.

You will be deceived if you look only to the appearance of men. You will be disappointed if you seek comfort and gain in them. If you seek Jesus in all, you will surely find Him. If you seek yourself, you will find yourself—to your ruin. The man who does not seek Jesus does himself greater harm than the whole world and all his enemies could ever do.

Chapter 8: Intimacy With Jesus

When Jesus is near, all is well and nothing seems difficult. When He is absent, all is hard. When Jesus does not speak within, all other comfort is empty. If He says only a word, it brings great consolation.

Did not Mary Magdalene rise at once from her weeping when Martha said to her: "The Master is come, and calleth for thee"? [John 11:28] Happy is the hour when Jesus calls one from tears to joy of spirit.

How dry and hard you are without Jesus. How foolish and vain if you desire anything but Him. Is it not a greater loss than losing the whole world? What can the world give you? Life without Jesus is a relentless hell. Living with Him is a sweet paradise. If Jesus be with you, no enemy can harm you.

He who finds Jesus finds a treasure; a good above every good. He who loses Him loses more than the whole world. The man who lives without Jesus is the poorest of the poor. No one is so rich as the man who lives in His grace.

It is an art to know how to converse with Jesus, and wisdom to know how to keep Him. Be humble and peaceful, and Jesus will be with you. Be devout and calm, and He will remain with you. You may drive Him away and lose His grace if you turn to the world. If you drive Him away and lose Him, whom will you seek as a friend? You cannot live well without a friend, and if Jesus be not your friend above all, you will be sad and desolate. You are acting foolishly if you trust or rejoice in any other. Choose the opposition of the whole world rather than offend Jesus. Of all those who are dear to you, let Him be your special love. Let all things be loved for the sake of Jesus, and for His own sake.

Jesus Christ must be loved with a special love for He alone is good and faithful. For Him and in Him you must love friends and foes alike, and pray to Him that all may know and love Him.

Never desire special praise or love, for that belongs to God alone who has no equal. Never wish that anyone's affection be centered in you, nor let yourself be taken up with the love of anyone. Let Jesus be in you and in every good man. Be pure and free within.

You must bring to God a clean and open heart if you wish to see how sweet the Lord is. You will never attain this happiness unless His grace prepares and draws you so you may forsake all things to be united with Him.

When the grace of God comes to a man he can do all things, but when it leaves him he becomes poor and weak, abandoned to affliction. In that condition he should not despair. On the contrary, he should calmly await the will of God and bear what befalls him in praise of Jesus Christ. After winter comes summer, after night, the day, and after the storm, a calm.

Chapter 9: How to Approach Comfort

It is not hard to spurn human comfort when we have the divine. It is a good thing to be able to live without divine or human comfort and for the honor of God. It is good to endure this exile of heart, and not seek oneself in anything; to think nothing of one's own merit.

Does it matter if at the coming of grace you are cheerful and devout? This is desired by all. He who the grace of God sustains travels easily. What wonder if he feel no burden when supported and led by the Almighty. We are glad to have something to comfort us. Only with difficulty does a man divest himself of self.

A martyr conquered the world because he despised everything in it that seemed pleasing to him. For love of Christ he suffered the loss of someone he loved. With love for the Creator he overcame the love of man and chose God's pleasure instead of human comfort. We must learn to part with a friend for the love of God. Do not take it to heart when you are deserted by a friend, knowing that in the end we must all be parted from one another.

A man must fight long and bravely against himself before he learns to master himself and to direct his desires toward God. When he trusts in himself, he seeks human consolation. The lover of Christ who pursues virtue does not fall back upon human comfort or seek sensual pleasure, but prefers trials and labors for the sake of Christ.

When spiritual consolation is given by God, receive it gratefully. Understand that it is His gift and not your merit. Do not exult, do not be presumptuous, but be humbler for the gift and more careful in your actions. For this hour will pass and temptation will come afterward.

When comfort is taken away, do not despair but wait humbly and patiently for God since He can restore your peace.

This is not strange to one who knows God's ways. Change of fortune often visited the prophets of old. There was one who declared: "In my prosperity I said: I shall never be moved.'" When grace was taken away, he said: "Thou didst hide Thy face, and I was troubled." He does not despair; rather he prays earnestly: "To Thee, O Lord, will I cry; and I will make supplication to my God." Later, he receives the fruit of his prayer, and says "The Lord hath heard, and hath had mercy on me: the Lord became my helper." How was he helped? "Thou hast turned," he says, "my mourning into joy, and hast surrounded me with gladness." [Ps. 29:7-12]

If this is the case with saints, we who are weak and poor ought not despair because we are both faithful and unfaithful. The spirit comes and goes according to His will. On this, Job declared: "Thou visits him early in the morning, and Thou proves him suddenly." [Job 7:18]

In what can I hope or in whom should I trust? Only in the mercy of God and hope of grace. I may have faithful friends, holy books and hymns, but these help little when I am abandoned by grace and left to myself. At such times there is no better solution than resignation to God's will.

I have never met a man so devout that he has not experienced absence of grace and reduction of faith. No saint has been without temptation. It is difficult to appreciate and contemplate God if you have not been tried by hardship.. Temptation usually precedes consolation, and heavenly consolation is promised to those proved by temptation. "To him that overcomes," says Christ, "I will give to eat of the Tree of Life." [Apoc. 2:7] Divine consolation is given to make a man brave in adversity. Temptation follows so he may not be proud of what he does.

The devil does not sleep, nor is the flesh dead. Never cease preparation for battle. On the right and left are enemies who never rest.

Chapter 10: Appreciate God's Grace

Why do you look for rest when you were born to work? Resign yourself to patience rather than comfort, to carrying your cross rather than enjoyment.

What man would not accept spiritual comfort and joy, which exceed earthly delights and pleasures of the body? The latter are often vain or base, while spiritual joys born of virtue and infused by God in pure minds are pleasant and noble.

Temptation is always near and false freedom and overconfidence in self are obstacles to the influence of heaven.

God does well in giving the grace of comfort, but man does evil in not returning everything gratefully to God. Gifts of grace cannot flow in us when we are ungrateful to the Giver. Grace is always given to him who is grateful, and what will be given to the humble will be taken from the proud.

I do not desire comfort which robs me of contrition, nor do I care for thoughts which lead to pride. Not all that is high is holy, nor all that is sweet is good, nor every desire pure, nor all that is dear to us, pleasing to God. I accept grace where I become humble, contrite and willing to renounce self.

The man who has been taught by grace and learns by its departure will not attribute good to himself, but will admit his poverty and emptiness. Give to God what is God's and credit yourself with what is yours. Give Him thanks for His grace, but place upon yourself the blame and punishment your sin deserves.

Take the lowest place and the highest will be given you, for the highest cannot exist apart from the lowest. The followers of Christ who are greatest before God are those who consider themselves the least. The more humble they are, the more glorious they are. Since they do not desire earthly glory, they are full of truth and heavenly glory. Established in God, they cannot be proud. They attribute to God what good they received. They seek no glory from one another but only what comes from God. They desire above all that He is praised in them and His church. This is their purpose.

Be grateful for the smallest gift and you will be worthy to receive a greater one. Consider the smallest gift as the greatest, and the contemptible as special. Focus on the dignity of the Giver, and no gift will appear small or worthless. Even though God gives punishment and hardship, accept them because He acts for our welfare in what He allows.

To keep the grace of God, be grateful when it is given and patient when it is absent. Pray that grace returns; and be cautious and humble so you do not lose it.

Chapter 11: Few Truly Love the Cross of Jesus

Jesus has many who love His kingdom, but few who bear His cross. He has many who desire comfort, but few who care for hardship. He finds many to share His table, but few to take part in His fasting. All desire to be happy with Him. Few wish to suffer for Him. Many follow Him to break bread, but few drink the chalice of His passion. Many revere His miracles; few approach the shame of the Cross. Many love Him as long as there is no hardship. Many praise and bless Him as long as they receive comfort.

If Jesus hides Himself and leaves them for a while, they complain or become dejected. Those who love Him for His sake and not for their comfort bless Him during trials and heartache as well as times of joy. Even if Jesus should never give them comfort, they would praise and give Him thanks. What power there is in pure love for Jesus--love that is free from self-interest and self-love.

Do not those who always seek comfort deserve to be called mercenaries? Do not those who always think of their own profit and gain prove that they love themselves rather than Christ? Where can a man be found who desires to serve God for nothing? Rarely indeed is a man so spiritual as to strip himself of all things. Who shall find a man so truly poor in spirit as to be free from every creature? His value is like that of treasure brought from distant lands.

If a man give all his wealth, it is nothing. If he gain all knowledge, if he have great virtue and much devotion, he still lacks a great deal. Especially the one thing that is most necessary to him. What is this one thing? That he leave all, forsake himself, and give up all desires. When he has done what ought to be done, let him consider it as nothing. Let him make little of what may be considered great. Let him in honesty call himself an unprofitable servant. Truth itself has said: "When you shall have done all these things that are commanded you, say: we are unprofitable servants.'" [Luke 17:10]

Then, he will be truly poor in spirit, and with the prophet may say: "I am alone and poor." [Ps. 24:16] No one is more wealthy than such a man. No one is more powerful. No one freer than he who knows how to leave all things and think of himself as the least of all.

Chapter 12: The Way of the Cross

To many the saying, "Deny thyself, take up thy cross and follow Me," [Matt. 16:24] seems hard, but it will be much harder to hear that final word: "Depart from Me, ye cursed, into everlasting fire." [Matt. 25:41] Those who hear the word of the cross and follow it need not fear they will hear of eternal damnation on the day of judgment. The sign of the cross will be in the heavens when the Lord comes to judge. All the servants of the cross who made themselves one with Christ will draw near with trust to the Judge.

Why do you fear to take up the cross when through it you can win a kingdom? In the cross is salvation. In the cross is life. In the cross is protection from enemies. In the cross is heavenly sweetness. In the cross is strength of mind. In the cross is joy. In the cross is virtue. In the cross is holiness. There is no salvation or hope of everlasting life but in the cross.

Take up your cross and follow Jesus, and you shall enter eternal life. He Himself opened the way before you in carrying His cross. Upon it He died for you, so that you might take up your cross and long to die upon it. If you die with Him, you shall live with Him. If you share His suffering, you shall share His glory.

In the cross is everything, and upon your dying on the cross depends everything. There is no other way to life and to true peace than the way of the cross. Go where you will, seek what you will. You will not find a higher way, or a less exalted but safer way, than the way of the cross. Arrange and order everything to suit your will and judgment, and still you will find that suffering must be borne, willingly or unwillingly. Thus, you will always find the cross.

Either you will experience bodily pain or you will undergo tribulation of spirit. At times you will be forsaken by God, at times troubled by those around you. Worse, you will often grow weary of yourself. You cannot escape, you cannot be relieved by comfort but must bear with it as long as God wills. He wishes you to learn to bear trials, to submit yourself to Him so you may become humble through suffering. No one understands the passion of Christ as the man who suffers.

The cross is always ready. It awaits you everywhere. No matter where you go, you cannot escape. Wherever you go, you take your self with you and can take up the cross. Turn where you will, you will find a cross in everything. You must have patience if you would find peace and obtain an eternal crown.

If you carry the cross, it will lead you to the place where there shall be no suffering, but on earth there will be. If you carry it unwillingly, you create a burden and increase the load. If you cast away one cross, you will find another and perhaps a heavier one. Do you expect to escape what no man can avoid? Which follower of Christ was without a cross or trial on this earth? Not even Jesus, our Lord, Whose every hour on earth knew the pain of His passion. "It behooveth Christ to suffer, and to rise again from the dead, . . . and so enter into his glory." [Luke 24:46, 26] How is it that you look for another way than the royal way of the holy cross?

The life of Christ was a cross and a martyrdom. Do you seek rest and enjoyment for yourself? You deceive yourself. You are mistaken if you seek anything but to suffer. The more spiritual progress a person makes, so much heavier will he find the cross, because as his love increases, the pain of his exile increases.

Such a man is not without hope of comfort, because he knows great reward is coming to him for bearing his cross. When he carries it willingly, every pang of tribulation is changed into hope of solace from God. The more the flesh experiences affliction, so much more is the spirit strengthened by grace. A man may be strengthened by his love of hardship in his desire to take up the cross of Christ. He may not wish to be without sorrow or pain, since he believes he will be acceptable to God if he is able to endure for His sake.

It is the grace of Christ through which frail flesh learns to love, and to gain what it shuns.

To love the cross, to bring the body to subjection, to flee honor, to endure contempt to despise self and wish to be despised, to suffer adversity and loss, to desire no prosperity on earth--this is not man's way. If you rely upon yourself, you can do none of these things. If you trust in God, strength will be given you from heaven. The world and flesh will be made subject to your word. You will not fear your enemy the devil, if you are armed with faith and the cross of Christ.

Set yourself to be a faithful servant of Christ, to bear bravely the cross of your Lord, who out of love was crucified for you. Be ready to suffer adversities. There is no way to evade the trials and sorrows of life but to bear them.

Drink the cup of the Lord with affection if you wish to share with Him and be His friend. Leave consolation to God. Let Him do as He pleases. Be ready to bear suffering and consider it consolation. The sufferings of this life are not worthy to be compared with the glory to come.

When you come to the point where suffering is sweet for the sake of Christ, then consider yourself fortunate, for you have found paradise on earth. As long as suffering bothers you and you seek to escape, so long will you be unfortunate. The tribulation you seek to evade will follow you everywhere. If you put your mind to the things you ought to consider, to suffering and death, you would soon be in a better state and find peace.

Although you may be taken to the third heaven with Paul, you are not protected against suffering. Jesus said: "I will show him how great things he must suffer for My name's sake." [Acts 9:16] To suffer remains your lot if you mean to love Jesus and serve Him.

If you were worthy to suffer something for the name of Jesus, what glory would be in store for you, what joy to the saints of God, what edification to those around you. For all men praise patience though there are few who wish to practice it.

With good reason, you ought to be willing to suffer a little for Christ since many suffer more for the world. Realize you must lead a dying life. The more a man dies to self, the more he begins to live for God.

No man is fit to enjoy heaven unless he has resigned himself to suffer hardship for Christ. Nothing is more acceptable to God, nothing more helpful for you on earth than to suffer willingly for Christ. If you had to make a choice, you ought to wish to suffer for Christ rather than enjoy many comforts. You would then be more like Christ. Our merit and progress consist not in pleasures and comforts but in enduring afflictions and sufferings.

If there were anything better or more useful for man's salvation than suffering, Christ would have shown it by word and example. But He clearly exhorts the disciples who follow Him and all who wish to follow Him to carry the cross. He says: "If any man will come after Me, let him deny himself, and take up his cross daily, and follow Me." [Luke 9:23]

When we have read and searched all that has been written, let this be the conclusion: it is through much suffering we must enter into the kingdom of God.

BOOK THREE: INTERNAL CONSOLATION
(Selections for the 21st Century)

Chapter 1: Conversation of Christ with the Faithful Soul

I will hear what the Lord God will speak in me. [Ps. 84:9] Blessed is the soul who hears the Lord speaking within her, who receives the word of comfort from His lips. Blessed are the ears that catch divine whispering, and pay no heed to the murmurings of this world. Blessed are the ears that listen, not to the worldly voice, but to the truth which teaches within. Blessed are the eyes which are closed to material things and are fixed upon those which are eternal. Blessed are they who look inward and try to understand mysteries and meaning. Blessed are they who give their time to God, and who cut themselves from the obstacles of the world.

Consider these things, my soul, and close the door of your senses, so that you can hear what God speaks within you. "I am your salvation," says your Beloved. "I am your peace and your life. Remain with Me and you will find peace. Dismiss all passing things and seek the eternal. What are all temporal things but snares? And what help will all creatures be able to give you if you are deserted by the Creator?" Leave all these things and make yourself pleasing and faithful to your Creator so that you may attain true happiness.

Chapter 4: Walk Before God in Humility and Truth

The Voice of Christ

My child, walk before Me in truth, and seek Me in the simplicity of your heart. He who walks before Me in truth shall be defended from evil, and the truth shall free him from seducers and from the slanders of wicked men. If the truth has made you free, then you shall be free, and you shall not care for the vain words of men.

The Disciple

O, Lord, it is true. I ask that it be with me as You say. Let your truth teach me. Let it guard me, and keep me safe to the end. Let it free me from evil desire and inappropriate loves. I shall walk with You in great freedom of heart.

The Voice of Christ

I shall teach you those things which are right and pleasing. Consider your sins with displeasure and sorrow. Never think yourself to be special because of your good works. You are a sinner. You are subject to passions and entangled in them. You tend toward nothing of worth. You fall quickly, are quickly overcome, troubled and undone. You have nothing in which you can glory, but you have many things for which you should think yourself vile. You are weaker than you can comprehend. Let none of the things you do seem great to you. Let nothing seem important or precious or desirable except that which is everlasting. Let the eternal truth please you above all, and let your unworthiness displease you. Fear nothing, abhor nothing, and flee from nothing as you do your vices and sins. These should be more unpleasant for you than any material loss.

Some men walk before Me without sincerity. Led on by curiosity and arrogance they wish to know My secrets and to understand exalted things of God, and neglect themselves and their salvation. Through their pride and curiosity, and because I am against them, such men often fall into temptations and sins.

Fear the judgment of God and wrath of the Almighty. Do not discuss the works of the Most High, but examine your sins; in what matters you have offended and what things you have neglected.

Some carry their devotion only in books, some in pictures, some in outward signs and figures. Some have Me on their lips when there is little of Me in their hearts. Others, with understanding and pure desires, long for eternal things. They are unwilling to hear of worldly matters, and with reluctance serve the necessities of nature. They sense what the Spirit of truth speaks within. He teaches them to despise earthly things and to love those of heaven, to neglect the world, and desire heaven daily.

Chapter 5: The Wonderful Effect of God's Love

The Disciple

I bless You, O heavenly Father, Father of my Lord Jesus Christ, for remembering me, a poor creature. Thanks to You, O Father of mercy, God of all comfort, Who refresh me, who am not worthy. I bless and glorify You with Your Son and the Holy Spirit, forever and ever.

Lord God, my holy Lover, when You come into my heart, all that is within me will rejoice. You are my glory and the exultation of my heart. You are my hope and refuge in the day of my tribulation. Because my love is weak and my virtue imperfect, I must be strengthened and comforted by You. Visit me often and teach me Your discipline. Free me from evil passion and cleanse my heart of inappropriate desire. Heal and purify me so I may be fit to love, strong to suffer and firm to persevere.

Love is an excellent thing, a very great blessing. It makes every difficulty easy, and bears wrongs with equanimity. It bears a burden without pain and renders sweet what is bitter. The noble love of Jesus spurs to great deeds and excites longing for what is more perfect. Love tends to rise. It will not be held down. Love wishes to be free and separated from worldly desires. Its sight will not be obstructed, or entangled in earthly matters or overcome by adversity.

Nothing is sweeter than love, nothing stronger or higher or wider. Nothing is more pleasant, fuller or better in heaven or on earth. Love is born of God and cannot rest except in God, Who is above all created things.

One who is in love flies, runs and rejoices. He is free, not bound. He gives all and possesses all because he rests in one sovereign Good, Who is above all things, and from Whom every good flows and proceeds. He does not look to the gift but turns himself to the Giver.

Love knows no limits. Love feels no burden, thinks nothing of troubles, attempts more than it is able and does not complain of impossibility. It believes it can do all things. For this reason, it is able to accomplish much, performing where he who does not love fails and falls.

Love is watchful. Sleeping, it does not slumber. Wearied, it is not tired. Pressed, it is not limited. Alarmed, it is not confused. Like a living flame, a burning torch, it forces its way upward and passes unharmed through every obstacle.

If a man loves, he will know the sound of this voice. For this warm affection of soul is a loud voice crying in the ears of God. It says: "My God, my love, You are all mine and I am all Yours. Give me more love, that I may learn to taste with my heart how sweet it is to love, how sweet to be dissolved in love and bathe in it. Let me be rapt in love. Let me rise above self in fervor and wonder. Let me sing the hymn of love. Let me follow You, my Love, to the heights. Let my soul exhaust itself in praising You, rejoicing out of love. Let me love You more than myself. Let me not love myself except for Your sake. In You let me love all those who truly love You, as the law of love, which shines forth from You, commands."

Love is swift, sincere, kind, pleasant and delightful. Love is strong, patient and faithful, prudent, long-suffering and manly. Love is never self-seeking, for when a person seeks himself he falls from love. Love is circumspect, humble and upright. It is neither soft nor light, nor focused upon vain things. It is sober and chaste, firm and quiet, guarded in all the senses. Love is subject and obedient to superiors. It is mean and contemptible in its own eyes, and devoted and thankful to God. It trusts and hopes in God even when difficult, for there is no living in love without sorrow. He who is not ready to suffer and be resigned to the will of the Beloved is not worthy to be called a lover. A lover must embrace what is difficult and bitter for the sake of the Beloved. He should not turn away from Him because of adversities.

Chapter 14: Consider God's Majesty and Do Not Become Proud

The Disciple

You thunder forth Your judgments over me, Lord. You shake my bones with fear and trembling, and my soul is afraid. I stand in awe as I consider that the heavens are not pure in Your sight. If You found wickedness in the angels and did not spare them, what will become of me? Stars have fallen from heaven. I who am but dust; how can I be presumptuous? They whose deeds seemed worthy of praise have fallen into the depths. I have seen those who ate the bread of angels delighting themselves with the husks of swine.

There is no holiness if You withdraw Your hand, Lord. There is no wisdom if You cease to guide. No courage if You cease to defend. No chastity is secure if You do not guard. Our vigilance avails nothing if Your watchfulness does not protect. Left to ourselves we sink and perish. Visited by You we are lifted up and live. We are unstable, but You make us strong. We grow lukewarm, but You inflame us.

How humbly and lowly should I think of myself. How little I should regard anything that seems good in me. How profoundly I should submit to Your judgment, Lord, where I find myself to be but nothing.

O impassable sea, where I find myself to be nothing. Where is glory's hiding place? Where can there be trust in my virtue? All pride is swallowed up in the depths of Your judgments upon me.

What is flesh in Your sight? Shall the clay glory against Him that formed it? How can he whose heart is subject to God be lifted up by pride? The whole world will not make him proud who has been subjected to truth. Nor shall he who has placed his hope in God be moved by flatterers. They who speak are nothing. They will pass away with the sound of their words, but the truth of the Lord remains forever.

Chapter 15: How One Should Speak and Feel

The Voice of Christ

My child, this is the way you must speak on every occasion: "Lord, if it be pleasing to You, so be it. If it be to Your honor, Lord, be it done in Your name. Lord, if You see that it is expedient and profitable for me, then grant that I may use it to Your honor. But if You know that it will be harmful to me, and of no benefit to the welfare of my soul, then take this desire away from me."

Not every desire is from the Holy Spirit, even though it may seem right and good. It is difficult to be certain whether it is a good or bad spirit which prompts one to do one thing or another. It is difficult even to know whether you are being moved by your own spirit. Many who seemed at first to be led by a good spirit have been deceived.

Whatever the mind sees as good, ask in fear of God and humility of heart. Above all, commit the whole matter to God with true resignation, and say: "Lord, You know what is better for me. Let this be done or that be done as You please. Grant what You will, as much and when You will. Do with me as You know best, as will please You and be for Your honor. Place me where You will and deal with me freely. I am in Your hand. Turn me whichever way You will. Behold, I am Your servant, ready to obey in all. Not for myself do I desire to live, but for You. Would that I could do this well."

A Prayer for the Will of God

Grant me Your grace, O merciful Jesus, that it may be with me. Work with and remain with me to the end. Grant that I may desire what is most pleasing to You. Let Your will be mine. Let my will follow and agree with Yours. Let my will be one with Yours, and let me be unable to do anything but what You will. Grant that I may die to all things in this world, and for Your sake to love to be despised and unknown in this life. Give me above all the desire to rest in You. In You, let my heart have peace. You are peace. You alone are its rest. Without You all things are difficult and troubled. In this peace that is in You, the Most High, the everlasting Good, I will sleep and take my rest. Amen.

Chapter 16: True Comfort Is Found in God Alone

The Disciple

Whatever I can desire or imagine for my own comfort I look for not here but in eternity. If I should have all the world's comforts and could enjoy all its delights, it is certain they could not endure for long. My soul, you cannot enjoy comfort or delight except in God, the Consoler of the poor and the Helper of the humble. My soul, wait for the divine and you will have all things in heaven. If you desire earthly things too much, you will lose those which are everlasting and heavenly. Use temporal things but desire eternal things. You cannot be satisfied with temporal goods because you were not created to enjoy them.

Even if you possessed all created things you could not be happy and blessed. Your blessedness and happiness occurs in God who created all things. It is not happiness as seen and praised by lovers of the world, but that for which the good and faithful servants of Christ wait. It is a happiness which the spiritual and pure of heart, whose conversation is in heaven, may sometimes have an understanding.

Vain and brief is all human comfort. That which is received from the truth is blessed and true. The devout man carries Jesus everywhere with him, and he says to Him: "Be with me, Lord Jesus, in every place and at all times. Let this be my comfort, to be willing to forego all human consolation. If Your consolation be wanting, let Your will and just trial be my greatest comfort. For You will not always be angry, nor will You threaten forever."

Chapter 17: Place All Cares in God

The Voice of Christ

My child, allow me to do what I will with you. I know what is best for you. You think as a man. You feel in many things as human desire persuades.

The Disciple

Lord, what You say is true. Your care for me is greater than the care I can take of myself. He who does not cast his care upon You stands unsafely. If only my will remains right and firm toward You. Lord, do with me whatever pleases You. Whatever You do with me can only be good.

If You wish me to be in darkness, I shall bless You. If You wish me to be in light, again I shall bless You. If You stoop down to comfort me, I shall bless You. If You wish me to be afflicted, I shall bless You forever.

The Voice of Christ

My child, this is the attitude which you should have if you wish to walk with Me. You should be as ready to suffer as to enjoy. You should be as willing to be destitute and poor as rich and satisfied.

The Disciple

O Lord, I shall suffer willingly for Your sake whatever You wish to send me. I am ready to accept from You both good and evil alike, the sweet and the bitter, sorrow with joy. For all that happens to me I am grateful. Keep me from sin and I will fear neither death nor hell. Do not cast me out or blot me from the Book of Life. Then, whatever tribulation occurs will not harm me.

Chapter 21: Rest in God

The Disciple

Above all things and in all things, my soul, rest always in God. He is the everlasting rest of the saints.

Grant, loving Jesus, that I may seek my rest in You above every creature. Above health and beauty; above honor and glory; power and dignity; above knowledge and cleverness, riches and arts, joy and gladness; above all fame and praise, all sweetness and consolation. Above hope and promise, merit and desire; above the gifts and favors that You can give or pour down upon me. Above the joy and exultation that the mind can receive and feel. Above the angels and archangels and heavenly host; above all things visible and invisible. May I seek my repose in You above all that is not You, my God.

You, my God, are above all things the best. You alone are most high, most powerful. You are most sufficient and satisfying, You are most sweet and consoling. You alone are most beautiful and loving, You are noble and glorious above all things. In You is every perfection that has been or ever will be. Whatever You give me besides Yourself, whatever You reveal to me about Yourself, and whatever You promise, is small and insufficient when I do not see and fully enjoy You alone. My heart cannot rest or be fully content until, rising above all gifts and every created thing, it rests in You. [Augustine, Confessions, i. 1]

Who, O most beloved Spouse, Jesus Christ, most pure Lover, Lord of all creation, who shall give me the wings of true liberty that I may fly to rest in You? When shall freedom be given me to see how sweet You are, my God? When shall I make myself within You? Because of Your love, may I feel, not myself, but You alone. I often grieve over my unhappiness. Many evils befall me, often disturbing me, making me sad and overshadowing me, often hindering, distracting and entangling me. I neither have access to You nor enjoy the embraces which are for the blessed. Let my desolation here on earth move You.

O Jesus, Splendor of eternal glory, Consolation of the pilgrim, with You my lips utter no sound and to You my silence speaks. How long will my Lord delay His coming? Let Him come to His servant and make him happy. Let Him put forth His hand and take this miserable creature from his anguish. O come, for without You there will be no happy hour, because You are my happiness and without You my table is empty. I am wretched, imprisoned and weighted down until You fill me with the Your presence. Restore me to liberty, and show me a friendly countenance. Let others seek what they will, but nothing pleases me or will please me but You, my God, my Hope, my everlasting Salvation. I will not be silent. I will not cease praying until Your grace returns to me and You speak to me, saying: "Behold, I am here. I have come to you because you have called Me. Your tears and the desire of your soul, your humility and contrition of heart have brought Me to you."

Lord, I have called You and desired You. I have been ready to give up all things for Your sake. You first spurred me to seek You. May You be blessed, O Lord, for having shown this goodness to Your servant according to Your mercies.

What more is there for Your servant to say? Unless, with his iniquity in mind, he humbles himself before You? Nothing among all the wonders of heaven and earth is like You. Your works are exceedingly good, Your judgments true, and Your providence rules the universe. May You be praised and glorified, O Father. Let my lips and my soul and all created things praise and bless You.

Chapter 23: Four Principles Which Bring Great Peace

The Voice of Christ

My child, I will teach you now the way of peace and true liberty.

1. Seek to do the will of others and not your own.

2. Choose to have less rather than more.

3. Seek the last place and to be beneath all others.

4. Wish and pray that the will of God be carried out in you.

Those with these attitudes will enter into peace and rest.

The Disciple

O Lord, this discourse of Yours contains much perfection. It is short in words but full of meaning and fruit. Certainly, if I could keep it faithfully, I should not be easily disturbed. As often as I find myself troubled and dejected, I find that I have departed from this teaching. You, Who can do all things, and Who always love what is for my welfare, give me grace that I may keep Your words and accomplish my salvation.

A Prayer Against Bad Thoughts

O Lord, be not far from me. O my God, help me, for thoughts and great fears have risen within me, afflicting my soul. How shall I escape them unharmed? How shall I disperse them?

"I will go before you," says the Lord, "and will humble the great ones of the earth. I will open the doors of the prison, and will reveal to you hidden secrets."

Do as You say, Lord, and let all evil fly from Your face. This is my hope and my only comfort: to fly to You in all suffering, to confide in You, and to call on You from the depths of my heart and to wait patiently for Your comfort.

A Prayer for Enlightening the Mind

Enlighten me, Jesus, with the brightness of light, and take away all darkness from my heart. Restrain my wandering thoughts and suppress the temptations which attack me. Fight for me, and vanquish these beasts, the desires of the flesh, so that peace may come through Your power and so Your praise may resound in the holy courts. Command the winds and the tempests. Say to the sea: "Be still," and to the north wind, "Do not blow," and there will be a calm.

Send forth Your light and Your truth to shine on the earth, for I am empty and formless until You illumine me. Pour out Your grace and shower my heart with heavenly dew. Open the springs of devotion to water the earth, that it may produce the best of fruit. Lift up my heart which is pressed down by sin, and direct my desire to heavenly things. Having tasted the sweetness of eternal happiness, let me find no pleasure in thinking of earthly things.

Snatch me up and deliver me from the passing comfort of creature. No created thing can fully quiet and satisfy my desires. Join me to Yourself in an inseparable bond of love; because You alone can satisfy him who loves You. Without You, all things are worthless.

Chapter 24: Avoid Inappropriate Curiosity About Others' Lives

The Voice of Christ

My child, do not be curious. Do not trouble yourself with idle concerns. Follow Me. What is it to you if a man is such, if another does or says this or that? You will not have to answer for others, but you will have to give an account of yourself. Why do you meddle in their affairs?

Behold, I know all men. I see everything that is done under the sun, and I know how matters stand with each. What is in his mind and heart, and the end to which his intention is directed. Commit all things to Me, and keep yourself in peace. Let him who is disturbed be as restless as he will. Whatever he has said or done will fall upon himself, for he cannot deceive Me.

Do not be anxious for a great name, for the close friendship of many, or for the affection of men. These things cause distraction and darkness around the heart. I would speak My word and reveal My secrets to you, if you would watch diligently for My coming and open your heart to Me. Be prudent. Watch in prayer, and in all things humble yourself.

Chapter 26: Obtain Freedom Through Prayer

The Disciple

It is the mark of a perfect man, Lord, never to let his mind relax in attention to heavenly things, and to pass through many cares as though he had none. He should do so not as a lazy man, but through exercise of a free mind to show no inappropriate desires.

Keep me, from the cares of this life, so I do not become entangled in them. Keep me from needs of the body, so I am not ensnared by pleasure. Keep me from depression and anxiety, so I am not broken by hardship and overcome. I do not ask deliverance from things which my vanity desires, but from miseries which oppress my soul and keep me from entering a freedom of spirit within You.

My God, make bitter all the carnal comforts that draw me from love of the eternal and lures me by the sight of some delightful good in the present. Let not flesh and blood conquer me. Let not the world and its brief glory deceive me, nor the devil trip me by his craftiness. Give me courage to resist, patience to endure, and constancy to persevere. Give me the soothing ointment of Your spirit rather than the consolations of the world. In place of carnal love, infuse in me the love of Your name.

Behold, eating, drinking, clothing, and other needs that sustain the body may be burdensome. Grant me grace to use such comforts in moderation and not become entangled in desire for them. It is not lawful to cast them aside completely, for nature must be sustained. Your holy law forbids us to demand superfluous things and things that are simply for pleasure. In these matters, let Your hand guide me, so that I may not overstep the law.

Chapter 27: Love of Self Greatest Obstacle in Life

The Voice of Christ

My child, you should give all for Me, and in no way belong to yourself. You must know that self-love is more harmful to you than anything else. In proportion to the love and affection you have for a thing, it can cling to you more or less. If your love is pure, simple and well ordered, you will not be a slave to anything. Do not covet what you may not have. Do not possess anything that can hinder or rob you of freedom.

It is strange that you do not commit yourself to Me with your whole heart, together with all that you can desire or possess. Why are you consumed with foolish sorrow? Why are you wearied with unnecessary care? Be resigned to My will and you will suffer no loss.

If you seek this or that, if you wish to be in this place or another, to have more ease and pleasure, you will never rest or be free from care. Defects are found in everything and someone will vex you everywhere. To obtain and multiply earthly goods will not help you. Rather, despise them and root them out of your heart. This is true not only of money and wealth, but also of desire for honor and empty praise, all of which will pass away.

The place matters little if the fervor is not there. Peace will not be lasting if it is sought from the outside. If your heart has no true foundation in Me, you may change, but will not better yourself. You will find again what you fled and worse.

A Prayer for Cleansing the Heart and Obtaining Heavenly Wisdom

Strengthen me with Your holy spirit, O God. Give me power to be strong, to empty my heart of all vain care and anxiety. Let me not be drawn away by desires, for precious things or mean ones. Let me look upon everything as passing, and upon myself as soon to pass away. There is nothing lasting under the sun. All is vanity and affliction of spirit.

Give me, Lord, wisdom to seek and find You, to enjoy and love You more than anything. Help me consider other things as they are, as Your wisdom has ordered them. Grant me prudence to avoid the flatterer and to be patient with him who disagrees with me. It is wise not to be moved by the sound of words, or give ear to the wicked and flattering siren.

Chapter 32: Pursue Self-Denial and Renunciation

The Voice of Christ

My child, you can never be truly free unless you renounce self, for all who seek their own interest and who love themselves are prisoners. They are disturbed by envy and curiosity. They search for ease and not the things of Christ. They pursue and create what will not last. Anything not of God will fail in the end.

Hold to this advice: give up your desires and you will find rest. Think of it in your heart, and when you have put it into practice you will understand all things.

The Disciple

But this, Lord, is not the work of a day. Nor is it child's play. In this short sentence is included the perfection of the holy.

The Voice of Christ

My child, do not be dismayed when you hear of the pure. Rather, you ought to be motivated toward the sublime, and to seek holiness.

I wish you had progressed to where you no longer loved self but awaited My bidding. You would please Me and your life would pass in peace and joy. But you have many things which you must give up. Unless you resign them to Me, you will not obtain what you seek.

"I counsel thee to buy of me gold, fire-tried, that thou may be made rich" [Apoc. 3:18] --rich in heavenly wisdom which tramples what is low. Put aside earthly wisdom and human self-complacency.

I have said: exchange what is precious among men for what is considered contemptible. True heavenly wisdom, to not think highly of self and to not seek glory on earth, seems small and is easily forgotten. Men praise it with their mouths but are far from it in their lives. Heavenly wisdom is a pearl of great price, which is hidden from many.

Chapter 33: Focus on Christ

The Voice of Christ

My child, do not trust in feelings, for they will give way to others. As long as you live you will be subject to change. You will become merry and sad, peaceful and disturbed, devout and not, diligent and lazy, grave and flippant.

A wise man pays no attention to changing feelings, to fickleness. His focus is on his proper and desired end. He can stand undivided and unshaken with his focus on Me, even in the midst of volatile events. The purer his focus, the greater his constancy as he passes through storms.

Your focus may grow hazy and dim because it is attracted to new and delightful things. It is hard to find one who is free from other interests and self-seeking. People came to Bethany to Martha and Mary not for Jesus' sake alone, but to see Lazarus.

Your focus must be clear and single and right. It must be directed toward Me, despite all objects which interfere.

Chapter 35: No Escape from Hardship; Seek God

The Voice of Christ

My child, in this life you are never safe. As long as you live the weapons of the spirit will be necessary. You dwell among enemies. You are subject to attack from the right and the left. If you do not guard yourself with the shield of patience, you will not remain long unscathed.

Set your heart on Me, with a will to suffer for My sake, and you will be able to bear the heat of battle and win the crown of the blessed. Pass through battle bravely, with a firm hand for what stands in your way. Heavenly bread is given to those who triumph. Misery remains for those who are too lazy to fight.

If you look for rest in this life, how will you obtain everlasting rest? Have an attitude of pursuing patience rather than rest. Seek peace, not on earth but in heaven, and not in men or creatures but in God. For the love of God you should undergo all cheerfully: labors and sorrows, temptations and trials, anxieties, weaknesses, necessities, injuries, slanders, rebukes, humiliations, confusions, discipline and contempt. These assist virtue. These are the trials of Christ's disciples. These form the heavenly crown. With brief labor on earth, I will gain an everlasting crown, and with brief hardship, glory that is eternal.

You will not always have spiritual comforts that you desire. Saints did not always have them. Instead, they had afflictions, temptations and great desolation, and bore them patiently. They placed their confidence in God and not themselves. They knew the sufferings of this life are not to be compared with the glory that is to come. Do you wish to have immediately what others have worked for with tears and great labor?

Wait for God, act bravely and have courage. Do not lose trust. Do not turn back but devote your body and soul to God's glory. I will reward you well. I will be with you in every tribulation.

Chapter 36: How to Approach the Judgment of Man

The Voice of Christ

My child, trust in God and do not fear the judgment of men when conscience tells you that you are upright and innocent. It is good and blessed to suffer such things. They will not weigh heavily on the humble heart that trusts in God. Many men say many things, and therefore little faith is to be put in them.

It is impossible to satisfy all men. Paul tried to please all in the Lord, and became all things to all men, yet he did not have undue respect for their opinions. He labored for the edification and salvation of others, but he could not escape being judged and despised by others. He committed all to God Who knows all things, and defended himself by his patience and humility against the tongues of those who spoke unjustly or thought foolish things and lies, or made accusations against him. Sometimes, he did answer them, but only so his silence would not mislead the weak.

Who are you that you should be afraid of mortal man? Today he is here, tomorrow he is not seen. Fear God and you will not be afraid of men. What can anyone do to you by word or injury? He hurts himself rather than you, and no matter who he may be he cannot escape the judgment of God. Keep God before your eyes, and do not quarrel with peevish words.

If it seems that you suffer undeserved shame, do not worry about it and do not lessen your crown through impatience. Look to heaven, to Me, Who has power to deliver you from disgrace and injury, and to reward everyone according to his works.

Chapter 37: Renounce the Self to Obtain Freedom

The Voice of Christ

My child, renounce the self and you shall find Me. Give up your own self-will and your possessions, and you shall always gain. Once you resign yourself, greater grace will be given you.

The Disciple

How often, Lord, shall I resign myself? And in what shall I forsake myself?

The Voice of Christ

Always, at every hour, in small matters as well as great; excepting nothing. In all things I wish you to be stripped of self. How can you be mine or I yours unless you eliminate your own will inwardly and outwardly? The sooner you do this the better for you, and the more fully and sincerely you do it the more you will please Me and the greater gain you will merit.

There are some who resign themselves, but with reservations. They do not trust fully in God and therefore they try to provide for themselves. Others, at first offer all, but afterward are assailed by temptation and return to what they have renounced, and make no progress in virtue. These will not reach the true freedom of a pure heart or the grace of happy friendship with Me. They must first resign themselves fully, and daily sacrifice themselves. Without this no fruitful union will last.

I have said to you often: forsake yourself, renounce yourself and you shall enjoy great inward peace. Give all for all. Ask nothing, and demand nothing in return. Trust purely and without hesitation in Me, and you shall possess Me. You will be free of heart, and darkness will not overwhelm you.

Strive and pray and desire this: to be stripped of all selfishness and naked to follow the naked Jesus. Die to self and live forever for Me. All vain imaginations, all wicked disturbances and superfluous cares will vanish. Inappropriate fears and desires will leave you.

Chapter 43: Beware Worldly Knowledge

The Voice of Christ

My child, do not let the fine sounding and subtle words of men deceive you. The kingdom of heaven consists not in talk but in virtue. Attend to My words which kindle the heart and enlighten the mind. They will result in contrition and comfort. Never read them for the purpose of appearing learned or wise. Apply yourself to eliminating your vices. This will benefit you more than understanding difficult questions.

Though you have read and learned much, it will always be necessary for you to return to this principle: I am He who teaches man knowledge, and to the little ones I give a clearer understanding than can be taught by man. He to whom I speak will soon be wise and his soul will profit. Woe to those who inquire about many curiosities, and care little about the way they serve Me.

The time will come when Christ, the Teacher of teachers, the Lord of angels, will appear to examine the conscience of everyone. He will search Jerusalem with lamps, and the hidden things of darkness will be brought to light and men's tongues will be silenced.

I am He Who in one moment can enlighten a humble mind with an eternal truth and with more than could be learned by ten years school. I teach without noise of words or clash of opinions, without ambition for honor or confusion of argument.

I am He Who teaches man to despise earthly possessions and to loathe earthly things. Ask after the eternal, and hunger for heaven. Place all hope in Me, and desire nothing apart from Me. Love Me above all things. A certain man by loving Me learned divine truths and spoke wonders. He profited more by leaving alone certain things than by studying subtle questions.

To some I speak of common things, to others of special matters. To some I appear with signs and figures, and to others I appear in light and reveal mysteries. The voice of books is but a single voice, yet it does not teach all men alike. Within them, I am the Teacher and the Truth, the Examiner of hearts, the Knower of thoughts, the Promoter of acts, distributing to each as I see fit.

Chapter 46: Trust in God; Do Not Desire to Please Men

The Voice of Christ

My child, stand firm and trust in Me. What are words but words? They fly through the air but do not hurt like a stone. If you are guilty, consider how you would change. If you are not conscious of fault, bear it for God. It is little enough for you to endure words, since you are not strong enough to bear hard blows.

Why do small matters pierce you, unless you are carnal and pay more heed to men than you ought? You do not wish to be disciplined for your faults and you seek shelter in excuses because you are afraid of being despised. Look into yourself and you will see the world is alive in you, with a vain desire to please men. When you shrink from being reproved for your failings, it is plain that you are not humble or dead to the world. The world is not crucified in you.

Listen to My word, and you will not value ten thousand words of men. If every malicious thing that could be invented were said against you, what harm could it do if you ignored it all and gave it no more thought?

He who does not keep his heart, and who does not have God before him is easily moved by disparagement. He who trusts in Me, and has no desire to stand by his judgment will be free from fear of men. I am the judge and discerner of all secrets. I know how all things happen. I know who causes injury and who suffers it. With My permission it happened, that out of many hearts thoughts may be revealed. I shall judge the guilty and the innocent; but I will try them by secret judgment.

The testimony of man is often deceiving, but My judgment is true. It will stand and not be overthrown. It is hidden from many and made known to a few. It is never mistaken even though it does not seem right in the eyes of the unwise.

To Me you ought to come in every decision, not depending on your own judgment. The just man will not be disturbed, no matter what may befall him from God. Even if an unjust charge be made against him he will not be much troubled. Neither will he exult vainly if through others he is justly acquitted. He considers that it is I Who search the hearts of men, that I do not judge according to human appearances. What the judgment of men considers praiseworthy is often blameworthy in My sight.

The Disciple

O Lord God, just Judge, You Who know the weakness and depravity of men, be my strength and all my confidence. My own conscience is not sufficient. You know what I do not know. I ought to humble myself when I am accused and bear it meekly. Forgive me in Your mercy for my failures, and give me the grace of endurance. Better to me is Your mercy in obtaining pardon than the justice which I imagine in defending my conscience. Though I may not be conscious of any fault, I cannot justify myself. Without Your mercy no man living will be justified in Your sight.

Chapter 47: Work Faithfully and Bear Hardship For Eternity

The Voice of Christ

My child, do not let the labors which you have taken up for My sake break you. Do not let troubles cast you down, but in everything let My promise strengthen and console you. I am able to reward you beyond all means and measure.

You will not labor here long, nor will you always be oppressed by sorrows. Wait a little and you will see a speedy end of evil. The hour will come when all labor and trouble will be no more. All that passes with time is trivial.

What you do, do well. Work faithfully in My vineyard. I will be your reward. Write, read, sing, mourn, keep silence, pray, and bear hardship. Eternal life is worth these and greater battles. Peace will come on a day which is known to the Lord, and then there shall be no day or night but perpetual light, infinite brightness, lasting peace, and safe rest. You will not say: "Who shall deliver me from the body of this death?" nor will you cry: "Woe is me, because my stay is prolonged." Death will be banished, and there will be unfailing health. There will be no anxiety, but joy; and sweet, noble companionship.

If you could see the crowns of the saints in heaven, and the glory where they rejoice. They were once considered contemptible in this world and unworthy of life. You would humble yourself, and seek to be subject to all rather than to command one person. You would not desire the pleasant days of this life, but be glad to suffer for God. Consider it your greatest gain to be counted as nothing among men.

If these things appealed to you and penetrated into your heart, how could you dare to complain? All trials should be borne for the sake of everlasting life. The loss or gain of God's kingdom is no small matter.

Lift up your face to heaven. Behold Me, and with Me all My saints. They had great trials in life, but now rejoice. They are comforted. They are safe and at rest. They shall abide with Me for all eternity in My Father's kingdom.

Chapter 48: Christ and Eternity will Overcome Sin and Evil

The Disciple

O happy mansion of the city above. O bright day of eternity, which night does not darken, but which highest truth enlightens. O day, joyful and secure, which never changes to night. Oh, that this day shines forth, that these temporal things come to an end. It envelops the saints with heavenly brightness, but it appears far off as through a glass to us wanderers on the earth. The citizens of heaven know how joyful is that day, but the exiled sons of Eve mourn that this one is bitter and tedious.

The days of this life are short and evil, full of grief and distress. Man is defiled by sin, ensnared in passion, enslaved by fear, and burdened with care. He is distracted by curiosity and entangled in vanity, surrounded by error and worn by labor, oppressed by temptation, weakened by pleasure and tortured by want.

When will these evils end? When shall I be freed from the slavery of vice? When, Lord, shall I think of You alone? When shall I rejoice in You? When shall I be without hindrance, in liberty, free from grievance of mind and body? When will there be peace, undisturbed and secure, inward peace and outward peace, secured on every side? O good Jesus, when shall I stand to gaze upon You? When shall I contemplate the glory of Your kingdom? When will You be all in all to me? When shall I be with You in that kingdom of Yours, which You have prepared for Your beloved for all eternity?

I am left poor and exiled in a hostile land, where every day sees wars and misfortunes. Console my banishment, assuage my sorrow. My whole desire is for You. The solace of this world is a burden to me. I desire to enjoy You intimately, but I cannot gain it. I wish to cling to heavenly things, but temporal affairs and passions bear me down. I wish to be above all things, but I am forced by the flesh to be subject to them. I fight with myself, and am a burden to myself. My spirit seeks to rise up and my flesh to sink down. What suffering I endure when I consider heavenly things. When I pray, carnal thoughts rush upon me.

O my God, do not remove Yourself from me. Do not depart in anger from Your servant. Cast Your lightning and disperse my enemies. Send Your arrows and let the phantoms of the enemy be put to flight. Draw my senses toward You. Make me forget all worldly things. Grant me the grace to cast away all vicious imaginings. Help me so that no vanity may move me. Come, heavenly Sweetness, and let all impurity fly before Your face.

Pardon me and deal mercifully with me whenever I think of anything besides You in prayer. I confess that I am often distracted. I am not where I stand or sit. I am where my thoughts carry me. Frequently, my thoughts are where my love is. What naturally delights, or is by habit pleasing, comes to me quickly. You, Who are Truth itself, have plainly said: "Where your treasure is, there is your heart also." If I love heaven, I think of heavenly things. If I love the world, I rejoice at the happiness of the world and grieve at its troubles. If I love the flesh, I imagine things that are carnal. If I love the spirit, I delight in thinking of spiritual matters. Whatever I love, I am willing to speak and hear about.

Blessed is the man who for You, O Lord, dismisses all creatures, does violence to nature and crucifies the desires of the flesh. With serene conscience he can offer You a pure prayer and, having excluded all earthly things, becomes worthy to enter into the heavenly choirs.

Chapter 53: God's Grace is Not Given to the Worldly Minded

The Voice of Christ

My child, my grace is precious. It does not allow itself to be mixed with earthly comforts. Cast away obstacles to grace if you wish to receive it fully.

Retire within yourself. Love to dwell with yourself. Seek no man's conversation, but pour forth prayer to God that you may keep your mind contrite and your heart pure.

Consider the whole world as nothing. You cannot attend upon Me and at the same time take delight in worldly things. You must remove yourself from acquaintances and from dear friends, and keep your mind free of temporal comforts. Thus the Apostle Peter begs the faithful of Christ to keep themselves as strangers and pilgrims in the world. [1 Peter 2:11]

What confidence at death shall be his who is not attached to this world by affection. The sickly soul does not know what it is to have a heart separated from all things. Nor does the natural man know the freedom of the spiritual man. If he truly wishes to be spiritual, he must renounce strangers and friends, and be aware of his self.

If you completely conquer your self, you will more easily subdue all other things. The perfect victory is to triumph over self. He who holds himself in subjection that sensuality obeys reason and reason obeys Me, is truly his own conqueror and master of the world.

If you wish to climb to this high position you must begin like a man, and lay the ax to the root in order to tear out and destroy any hidden unruly love of self or earthly goods.

From the vice of self-love comes almost every other vice that must be uprooted. When this evil is vanquished, and brought under control, great peace and quiet will follow.

Because few labor to die entirely to self, they remain entangled in self and cannot be lifted in spirit above themselves. He who desires to walk freely with Me must eliminate earthly affections and not cling with selfish love or desire to any creature.

Chapter 54: Nature Versus Grace

The Voice of Christ

My child, pay attention to the movements of nature and grace. They move in contrary and subtle ways, and can scarcely be distinguished by anyone except a man who is spiritual and enlightened. Many men desire what is good and strive for what is good in words and deeds. For this reason the appearance of good deceives many.

Nature is crafty and attracts many, ensnaring and deceiving them while seeking itself. Grace walks in simplicity, turns away from even the appearance of evil, offers no deceits and does everything purely for God.

Nature is not willing to die, or to be kept down or to be overcome. Nor will it subdue itself or be made subject. Grace, on the contrary, strives for denial of self. She resists sensuality, seeks to be in subjection and has no wish to use her own liberty. She loves to be under discipline and does not desire to rule over anyone. She wishes to live and to always be under God for Whose sake she is willing to bow humbly to every human creature.

Nature works for its own interest and looks to the profit it can reap from another. Grace does not consider what is useful and advantageous to herself, but to what is profitable to many. Nature likes to receive honor and reverence. Grace attributes all honor and glory to God. Nature fears shame and contempt. Grace is happy to bear reproach for the name of Jesus. Nature loves ease and rest. Grace cannot bear to be idle and embraces labor willingly. Nature seeks to possess what is rare and beautiful, abhorring things that are cheap and coarse. Grace delights in simple, humble things, not despising those that are rough, nor refusing to be clothed in old garments.

Nature has regard for temporal wealth and rejoices in earthly gains. It is sad over a loss and irritated by a slight. Grace looks to eternal things and does not cling to the temporal. She is neither disturbed at loss nor angered by hard words. She has placed her treasure and joy in heaven where nothing is lost.

Nature is covetous, and receives more than it gives. It loves its own possessions. Grace is kind and openhearted. Grace shuns private interest, is contented with little, and judges it more blessed to give than to receive.

Nature is inclined toward creatures, toward its own flesh and vanities. Grace draws near to God and to virtue, renounces creatures, hates the desires of the flesh, restrains her wandering and blushes at being seen in public.

Nature likes to have comfort in which it can take sensual delight, but grace seeks consolation only in God. She finds her delight in the highest Good, above all visible things.

Nature does everything for its own gain and interest. It can do nothing without pay and hopes for its good deeds to receive their equal or better, or praise and favor. It is desirous of having its deeds and gifts highly regarded. Grace seeks nothing temporal, nor does she ask any payment but God alone. Of earthly necessities she asks no more than will serve to gain eternity.

Nature rejoices in many friends and kinsfolk, glories in noble position and birth, fawns on the powerful, flatters the rich and applauds those who are like itself. Grace loves even her enemies and is not puffed up at having many friends. She does not think highly of position or birth unless there is virtue there. She favors the poor in preference to the rich. She sympathizes with the innocent rather than the powerful. She rejoices with the true rather than the deceitful. She exhorts the good to strive for better gifts, to become like the Son of God by practicing virtue.

Nature is quick to complain of need and trouble. Grace is strong in suffering.

Nature turns all things back to self. It fights and argues for self. Grace brings all things back to God in Whom they have their source. To herself she ascribes no good, nor is she arrogant or presumptuous. She is not contentious. She does not prefer her own opinion to those of others. In every matter of sense and thought she submits to eternal wisdom and divine judgment.

Nature has a relish for knowing secrets and hearing news. It wishes to be seen and have many sensual experiences. It wishes to be known and to do things for which it will be praised and admired. Grace does not care to hear news or gossip, because this arises from the corruption of man. There is nothing new, nothing lasting on earth. Grace teaches restraint of senses, avoidance of self-satisfaction and show. She teaches humility, the hiding of deeds worthy of praise and admiration. She teaches the fruit of usefulness, the praise and honor of God. She will not have herself exalted, but desires that God Who bestows everything out of love be blessed in His gifts.

Grace is a supernatural light, a special gift of God, the proper mark of the elect and the pledge of everlasting salvation. It raises man from earthly things to love things of heaven. It makes a spiritual man of a carnal one.

The more nature is held in check and conquered, the more grace is given. Every day the interior man may be reformed by new visitations of the Holy Spirit.

Chapter 55: The Corruption of Nature and Power of Grace

The Disciple

O Lord, my God, Who created me in Your own image and likeness, grant me the grace which You have shown to be so great and necessary for salvation, that I may overcome my evil nature which is drawing me to sin and perdition. I feel in my flesh the law of sin contradicting the law of my mind and leading me to serve sensuality. I cannot resist the passions unless Your holy grace infused in my heart assists me.

There is need of Your great grace to overcome a nature prone to evil from youth. Through the first man, Adam, nature is fallen and weakened by sin, and the punishment of that stain has fallen upon all mankind. Nature itself, which You created good and right, is considered a symbol of vice and the weakness of corrupted nature. When left to itself it tends to evil and base things. The little strength remaining in it is like a spark hidden in ashes. That strength is natural reason which, surrounded by thick darkness, still has the power of judging good and evil, of seeing the difference between true and false. However, it is not able to fulfill all it approves and does not enjoy the full light of truth or soundness of desire.

My God, according to the inward man I delight in Your law, knowing that Your command is good, just, and holy. It proves the necessity of shunning all evil and sin. In the flesh I keep the law of sin, obeying sensuality rather than reason. The will to good may be present in me, but I do not know how to accomplish it. I often propose good things, but because grace to help my weakness is lacking, I give up at the slightest resistance. I know the way of perfection and see how I ought to act, but because I am pressed down by my corruption I do not rise to more perfect things.

O Lord, Your grace is necessary to begin any good deed, to carry it on to completion. Without grace I can do nothing, but with its strength I can do all things in You. Without heavenly Grace our merits are nothing and no gifts of nature are to be esteemed.

Before You, O Lord, no arts or riches, no beauty or strength, no wit or intelligence avail without grace. Gifts of nature are common to good and bad alike, but the gifts of Your elect should be grace and love. Those who are signed with grace and love may be given everlasting life by God. Without grace, no gifts of prophecy or miracles, and no exalted meditation can be considered anything. Not even faith or hope or other virtues are acceptable to You without Your grace and love.

O blessed grace which makes the poor in spirit rich in virtue, which renders him who is rich in many good things humble of heart, come upon me. Fill me with your comfort before my soul faints with weariness and spiritual dryness.

Let me find grace in Your sight. Your grace is enough for me, even though I obtain none of the things which nature desires. If I am tempted and afflicted with tribulations, I will fear no evil while Your grace is with me. This is my strength. This will give me counsel and help. This is more powerful than my enemies and wiser than the wise. This is the mistress of truth, the teacher of discipline, the light of the heart, the consoler in anguish, the banisher of sorrow, the expeller of fear, the nourisher of devotion, the producer of tears. What am I without grace, but dead wood, a useless branch, fit only to be thrown away?

Let Your grace go before me and follow me, O Lord, and make me always intent upon good works through Jesus Christ, Your Son.

Chapter 56: Deny the Self and Imitate Christ, Bearing His Cross

The Voice of Christ

My child, the more you depart from yourself, the more you will be able to enter into Me. As the giving up of external things brings internal peace, the forsaking of self unites you to God. I will have you learn perfect surrender to My will, without contradiction or complaint.

Follow Me. I am the Way, the Truth, and the Life. Without the Way, there is no going. Without the Truth, there is no knowing. Without the Life, there is no living. I am the Way which you must follow, the Truth which you must believe, the Life for which you must hope. I am the inviolable Way, the infallible Truth, the unending Life. I am the Way that is straight, the supreme Truth, the Life that is true, the blessed, the uncreated Life. If you abide in My Way you shall know the Truth, and the Truth shall make you free, and you shall attain everlasting life.

If you wish to enter into life, keep My commandments. If you will know the truth, believe in Me. If you will be perfect, sell all. If you will be My disciple, deny yourself. If you will possess the blessed life, despise this present life. If you will be exalted in heaven, humble yourself on earth. If you wish to reign with Me, carry the Cross with Me. Only true servants of the Cross find the life of blessedness and true light.

The Disciple

Lord Jesus, because Your way is narrow and despised by the world, grant that I may despise the world and imitate You. The servant is not greater than his Lord, nor the disciple above the Master. Let Your servant be trained in Your life, for there is my salvation and true holiness. Whatever else I read or hear does not fully refresh or delight me.

The Voice of Christ

My child, now that you know these things and have read them, happy will you be if you do them. He who has My commandments and keeps them is who loves Me. I will love him and show Myself to him, and he will sit down with Me in My Father's Kingdom.

The Disciple

Lord Jesus, as You have said, so be it, and what You have promised, let it be my lot to gain. I have received the cross from Your hand. I will carry it even unto death as You have laid it upon me. The life of a good man is a cross, but it leads to paradise. We have begun. We may not go back, nor may we give up.

Take courage, brethren, let us go forward together and Jesus will be with us. For Jesus' sake we have taken this cross. For Jesus' sake let us persevere. He will be our help as He is our leader and guide. Our King goes before us and will fight for us. Let us follow like men. Let no man fear any terrors. Let us be prepared to meet death valiantly in battle. Let us not allow our glory to be blemished by fleeing from the Cross.

Chapter 57: Do Not be Sad or Anxious

The Voice of Christ

My child, patience and humility in adversity are more pleasing to Me than comfort and devotion when things are going well.

Why are you saddened by something said against you? Even if it had been more you ought not to be affected. Let it pass. It is not the first, nor is it anything new, and if you live long it will not be the last.

You are manly enough as long as you meet no opposition. You give good advice to others, and you know how to strengthen them with words. But when unexpected tribulation comes to your door, you fail both in counsel and in strength. Consider your great weakness, which you experience so often in small matters. When these and like trials happen, they happen for your good.

Put it out of your heart as best you know how. If it has touched you, do not let it cast you down or confuse you for long. Bear it patiently if you cannot bear it cheerfully. Even though you bear it unwillingly and are indignant, restrain yourself and let no inappropriate words pass your lips at which the weak might be scandalized. The storm that is aroused will soon be quieted and your inward grief will be sweetened by returning grace. "I yet live," says the Lord, "ready to help you and to console you more and more, if you trust in Me and call devoutly upon Me."

Remain tranquil and prepare to bear greater trials. All is not lost even though you be troubled or tempted grievously. You are a man, not God. You are flesh, not an angel. How can you possibly expect to remain in the same state of virtue when the angels in heaven and the first man in paradise failed to do so? I am He Who rescues the afflicted and brings to My divinity those who know their own weakness.

The Disciple

Blessed be Your words, O Lord, sweeter to my mouth than honey and the honeycomb. What would I do in great trials and anxieties if You did not strengthen me with Your holy words? If I may attain to the haven of salvation, what does it matter what or how much I suffer? Grant me a good end. Grant me a happy passage out of this world. Remember me, my God, and lead me by the right way into Your kingdom.

Chapter 58: God is Inscrutable

The Voice of Christ

My child, beware of discussing why one person is forsaken and why that one is favored, or why one man is afflicted and another exalted. Such things are beyond human understanding and no reason or argument can fathom the judgments of God.

When the enemy puts such suggestions in your mind, or when curious persons raise questions about them, answer with the prophet: "Thou art just, O Lord, and righteous are Thy judgments"; [Ps. 119:137] and this: "The judgments of the Lord are true and wholly righteous." [Ps. 19:9] My judgments are to be feared, because they are incomprehensible to the understanding of men.

Similarly, do not inquire or argue about the merits of saints, as to which is more holy or which shall be greater in the kingdom of heaven. Such things breed strife and useless contention. They nourish pride and vainglory, envy and quarrels, when one proudly tries to exalt one saint over another. A desire to pry into such matters brings no fruit. I am the God not of dissension, but of peace; of that peace which consists in humility rather than in self-exaltation.

Some have a preference for one saint or another, but this preference is human and not divine. I am He who made all the saints. I gave them grace. I brought them to glory. I know the merits of each. I blessed them. I knew them before the ages. I chose them out of the world. They did not choose Me. I called them by grace. I drew them by mercy. I led them safely through temptations. I poured into them glorious consolations. I gave them perseverance and crowned their patience. I know the first and the last. I embrace them all with love. I am to be praised in all My saints. I am to be blessed above all things, and honored in each of them. I exalted and predestined they who did not have prior merits of their own.

He who despises one of the least of mine, does no honor to the greatest. I made both the small and the great. He who disparages one of my followers disparages Me and all others in the kingdom of heaven. They are all one through the bond of love. They have the same thought and will, and they love one another. What is a greater thing, they love Me more than themselves or their merits. Drawn beyond love of self, they are absorbed in love of Me, in Whom they rest. There is nothing that can draw them away, for they who are filled with eternal truth burn with unquenchable love.

Let carnal and sensual men who know only how to love their own selfish joys avoid arguing about God's saints. Such men subtract and add according to their inclination and not as it pleases God. In many this is ignorance, especially in those who are little enlightened and rarely love anyone with a spiritual love. They are strongly drawn by earthly affection and human friendship. Their imaginings of heavenly things are based on their understanding such earthly things. There is a great distance between what the imperfect imagine and what enlightened men contemplate through revelation from above.

Be careful, My child, of addressing matters beyond your understanding out of curiosity. Let it be your business and aim to be found within the kingdom of God even if you are the least. What value would knowledge of who is holy or great be to someone unless out of that knowledge he should humble himself before Me and rise up in greater praise of My name?

The man who thinks of the greatness of his sin, the smallness of his virtue and the distance between himself and the perfection of Christ acts more acceptably to God than one who argues about who is greater or less. It is better to invoke Christ with devout prayers and tears, and with a humble mind to beg His aid, than to search with inquisitiveness into secret knowledge.

Saints and followers of Christ do not glory in their own merit, for they attribute no good to themselves but all to Me. Out of My infinite love I gave all to them. They are filled with love of God and overflowing joy. No glory is wanting to them and they can lack no happiness. Those who follow Me are nearer, more beloved to Me and higher in glory when they humble themselves. You find it written that they cast their crowns before God, and fell down upon their faces before the Lamb, and adored Him Who lives forever.

Many ask who is greater in the kingdom of heaven when they do not know whether they will be numbered among the least. It is a great thing to be even the least in heaven where all are great because all shall be called the children of God. The least shall be as a thousand, and the sinner of a hundred years shall dic. When the disciples asked who should be greater in the kingdom of heaven they heard this response: "Unless you be converted and become as little children, you shall not enter into the kingdom of heaven. Therefore, whosoever shall humble himself as this little child, he is the greater in the kingdom of heaven." [Matt. 18:3, 4]

Woe to those who disdain to humble themselves with little children. The low gate of the heavenly kingdom will not permit them to enter. Woe to the rich who have their comforts on earth. When the poor enter God's kingdom, the rich will stand outside lamenting. Rejoice, you humble, and exult, you poor, for the kingdom of God is yours, if only you walk in truth.

Chapter 59: Hope and Trust In God Alone

The Disciple

What, Lord, is the trust I have in this life, or my greatest comfort among all that appears under heaven? Is it not You, my God, Whose mercies are without number? Where have I done well but for You? How could things go badly when You were present? I would rather be poor for Your sake than rich without You. I prefer to wander the earth with You than possess heaven without You. Where You are, there is heaven. Where You are not, there is death and hell. You are my desire and I must cry for You and sigh and pray. In none can I trust to help me in my necessities, but You alone. You are my hope. You are my confidence. You are my consoler, and faithful in every need.

All seek their own interests. You, Lord, place my salvation and my profit first, and turn all things to my good. Even though You allow my exposure to temptation and hardship, You order this for my good. You ought not be loved or praised less in hardship than if You filled me with heavenly comforts.

In You, O Lord, I place all my hope and refuge. On You I cast all my troubles and anguish. Whatever I have outside of

You I find to be weak and unstable. It will not serve me to have many friends, nor will powerful helpers be able to assist me, nor prudent advisers give useful answers, nor books of learned men console, nor precious substances win my freedom, nor any place, secret and beautiful though it be, shelter me, if You do not assist, comfort, console, instruct, and guard me. All things which seem to be for our peace and happiness are nothing when You are absent. Without You, none confer happiness.

You are the fountain of good, the height of life, the depth of all that can be spoken. To trust in You above all is the strongest comfort of Your servants.

My God, the Father of mercy, to You I look, in You I trust. Bless and sanctify my soul with a benediction, so that it may become Your holy dwelling and the seat of Your eternal glory. In this temple let nothing be found that offends Your majesty. In Your goodness and mercy look upon me and listen to the prayer of Your servant who is exiled from You and in the shadow of death. Protect and preserve the soul of Your servant among the dangers of this corruptible life. Direct him by Your grace through the way of peace to the land of everlasting light.

BOOK FOUR: AN INVITATION TO HOLY COMMUNION

(Selections for the 21st Century)

The Voice of Christ

Come to Me all you that labor and are burdened, and I will refresh you. [Matt 11:28] The bread which I give is My Flesh, for the life of the world. [John 6:52] Take you and eat. This is My Body which shall be delivered for you. Do this for the commemoration of Me. [1 Cor 11:24] He that eats My flesh and drinks My blood abides in Me and I in him. [John 6:57] The words that I have spoken to you are spirit and life. [John 6:64]

Chapter 1: Receive Christ with Reverence

The Disciple

These are Your words, O Christ, eternal Truth, though they were not spoken at one time nor written in one place. Because they are Yours and true, I must accept them with faith and gratitude. They are Yours and You have spoken them. They are mine because You have spoken them for my salvation. I accept them from Your lips that they may be more deeply impressed on my heart.

Words of such tenderness, so full of sweetness and love, encourage me. My sins frighten me and an unclean conscience thunders at me when approaching great mysteries like these. The sweetness of Your words invite me, but the multitude of my vices oppresses me.

You command me to approach You confidently if I wish to have a part of You, and to receive the food of immortality if I desire to obtain life and glory everlasting.

"Come to me," You say, "all you that labor and are burdened, and I will refresh you." [Matt. 11:28]

How sweet and kind to the ear of the sinner is the word by which You, my Lord God, invite the poor and needy to receive Your most holy Body! Who am I, Lord, that I should presume to approach You? Behold, the heavens cannot contain You, and yet You say: "Come, all of you, to Me."

What does this gracious honor and friendly invitation mean? How shall I dare to come; I who am conscious of no good on which to presume? How shall I lead You into my house; I who have so often offended in Your kindly sight? Angels and archangels revere You, the holy and the just fear You, and You say: "Come to Me: all of you." If You, Lord, had not said it, who would have believed it to be true? If You had not commanded, who would dare approach?

Noah, a just man, worked a hundred years building the ark that he and a few others might be saved. How can I prepare myself in one hour to receive with reverence the Maker of the world?

Moses, Your great servant and special friend, made an ark of incorruptible wood which he covered with purest gold in which to place Your laws. Shall I, a creature of corruption, dare so easily to receive You, the Maker of law and the Giver of life?

Solomon, the wisest of the kings of Israel, spent seven years building a magnificent temple in praise of Your name, and celebrated its dedication with a feast of eight days. He offered a thousand victims in Your honor and bore the Ark of the Covenant with trumpeting and jubilation. How shall I, unhappy and poorest of men, lead You into my house; I who scarcely can spend a half-hour devoutly?

O my God, how hard these men tried to please You. How little is all that I do. How short the time I spend in preparing for Communion. I am seldom wholly composed, and very seldom free from distraction. Surely in the presence of Your life-giving Godhead no unbecoming thought should arise and no creature possess my heart. I am about to receive as my guest, not an angel, but the very Lord of angels.

Great is the difference between the Ark of the Covenant with its treasures and Your most pure Body with its ineffable virtues. Great is the difference between these sacrifices of law which were figures of things to come and the offering of Your Body which was the fulfillment of all ancient sacrifices.

Why do I not long more ardently for Your adorable presence? Why do I not prepare myself with greater care to receive Your sacred gifts? Those holy patriarchs and prophets of old have shown such affectionate devotion for the worship of God.

The devout King David danced before the ark of God with all his strength in praise of You. He made musical instruments of many kinds. He composed psalms and ordered them sung with joy. He himself played upon the harp when moved by the grace of the Holy Ghost. He taught the people of Israel to praise God with all their hearts and to raise their voices every day to bless and glorify Him. If such devotion flourished in those days in praise of God before the Ark of the Covenant, what great devotion should I and all Christian people show in the presence of this Sacrament. What reverence should we show in receiving the Body of Christ itself.

Many people travel far to honor the relics of the saints, marveling at their deeds and at the building of magnificent shrines. They gaze upon and kiss the sacred relics encased in silk and gold. While You are actually present before me on the altar, my God, Saint of saints, Creator of men, and Lord of angels.

Often in looking at such things men are moved by curiosity and the novelty of the unseen. They take away little fruit for the transformation of their lives, especially when they go from place to place easily and without contrition. In the Sacrament of the altar You are wholly present, my God, the man Christ Jesus. In the Sacrament is obtained the realization of salvation, as often as God is devoutly received. We are not drawn by levity, curiosity or sensuality, but by faith, hope and love.

O God, hidden Creator of the world, how wonderfully You deal with us. How graciously You take care of those to whom You offer Yourself in this Sacrament. It surpasses all understanding. It attracts the hearts of the devout and inflames their love. Your faithful servants who give their life to transformation often receive in Holy Communion the grace of devotion and love of virtue.

There is a wonderful grace in the Sacrament which the faithful of Christ understand, which unbelievers and slaves of sin cannot experience. Spiritual grace is conferred, lost virtue restored, and beauty marred by sin is repaired. Its grace is so great that from the fullness of devotion not only the mind but the body feels filled with strength.

Our neglect and coldness is to be deplored and pitied when we are not moved to receive with fervor Christ in Whom is the hope of all who will be saved. He is our sanctification and redemption. He is our consolation in this life and the joy of the blessed in heaven. It is lamentable that many pay little heed to the Mystery which fills the heavens with joy and maintains the universe in being.

Blind and hard are the heart of a man that does not show regard for so wonderful a gift, but rather falls into carelessness from its regular use. If this holy Sacrament were celebrated in only one place in the world, with what great desire would men be attracted to that place. Now, communion is offered in many places, so that God's grace and love for men may be clear as communion is spread widely through the world.

Thanks be to You, Jesus, Who have seen fit to feed us poor sinners and exiles with Your precious Body and Blood, and to invite us with words from Your lips to partake of these Mysteries. "Come to Me, all you who labor and are burdened, and I will refresh you."

Chapter 2: God's Goodness and Love Are in the Sacrament of Communion

The Disciple

Trusting in Your goodness and mercy, O Lord, I come as one sick to the Healer. I come hungry and thirsty to the Fountain of life. I come as one in need to the King of heaven, a servant to his Lord, a creature to his Creator, a soul in desolation.

How is it that You come to me? Who am I that You should offer Yourself? How dare the sinner appear in Your presence? How do You condescend to come to the sinner? You know Your servant, and You know that he has nothing good in him that You should treat him so.

I confess my unworthiness. I acknowledge Your goodness. I praise Your mercy, and give thanks for Your love. It is by Your grace that You do it, not because of my merit. Your goodness ought to be known to me, so that love and humility may be born in me. Since this pleases You, I praise Your graciousness. I pray my sinfulness will not stand in the way.

Merciful Jesus, what great reverence, thanks and praise are due to You for the Sacrament.

What shall I think of this Communion, this approach to my Lord? I can never reverence You as I ought. Yet, I desire devoutly to receive You. I must humble myself completely in Your presence and exalt Your goodness above myself?

I praise You, my God, and extol You forever. I despise myself and cast myself before You. You are the Holy of holies. I am the scum of sinners. You serve me who am not worthy to look up to You. You come to me! You wish to be with me. You invite me to Your banquet. You give me heavenly food, the Bread of Angels, Yourself, the living Bread Who comes down from heaven and gives life to the world.

How Your love proceeds, and mercy shines forth. Great thanks and praise are due You for these gifts. How beneficial was Your design in the Sacrament; how pleasant the banquet when You gave Yourself.

Your work is admirable. Your power is great. Your truth is infallible. You spoke and all things were made. What you commanded was done. It is a wonderful thing, worthy of faith, overpowering human understanding. You, O Lord, my true God and man, are contained within the symbols of bread and wine, without being consumed by him who receives You.

You, the Lord of the universe, Who needs nothing, have wished to dwell in us through Your Sacrament. Keep my heart and body clean, so that with a spotless conscience I may be able to celebrate Your Mysteries. I can receive my salvation by what You ordained for Your honor and as an everlasting memorial.

Rejoice my soul, and give thanks to God for having left you a noble gift and consolation in this valley of tears. You are redeemed and become a part of Christ as often as you receive the Body of Christ. The love of Christ never lessens and His mercy is never exhausted.

You should prepare yourself by constantly renewing your heart and pondering the mystery of salvation. As often as you celebrate the Sacrament, it should seem as great to you as the day Christ was born on earth or crucified for the salvation of man.

Chapter 17: Receive Christ with Love and Desire

The Disciple

With greatest devotion and ardent love, with all affection and fervor of heart I wish to receive You, O Lord. Just as many saints and devout persons, pleased You with their holiness and devotion, and desired You in Communion.

My God, everlasting love, my final good, my happiness unending, I long to receive You with as strong a desire reverence as any saint. I am not worthy to have these sentiments of devotion, still I offer You the affection of my heart.

Whatever a God-fearing mind can conceive and desire, I offer to You with reverence and affection. I wish to keep nothing for myself but to offer to You myself and all that is mine.

O Lord, my Creator and my Redeemer, I long to receive You with reverence, praise, and honor, with gratitude, worthiness and love, with faith, hope, and purity. Your mother, the Virgin Mary, longed for and received You when she humbly and devoutly answered the angel who announced to her the mystery of the Incarnation: "Behold the handmaid of the Lord; be it done to me according to thy word." [Luke 1:38]

Your blessed precursor, John the Baptist, gladdened by Your presence, exulted in the Holy Ghost while yet in the womb of his mother. Afterward, seeing Jesus walking among men, he humbled himself and with devout love declared: "The friend of the bridegroom, who stands and hears him, rejoices with joy because of the bridegroom's voice." [John 3:29] I long to be inflamed with great and holy desire and to give myself to You with all my heart.

I offer to You the gladness of all devout hearts, their ardent affection and mental rapture, their supernatural illumination and heavenly vision. I offer to you the praises which have been celebrated by all creatures in heaven and on earth, that You may be praised and glorified forever.

Accept, O Lord, my promises of infinite praise and boundless benediction, which in Your ineffable greatness are due You. I render every day and every moment of time, and entreat all celestial spirits and the faithful to join me in giving You praise and thanks.

Let all people, races and tongues praise You and with the greatest joy and most ardent devotion magnify Your sweet and holy name. Let all who devoutly celebrate this Sacrament and receive it in the fullness of faith, find kindness and mercy in You. Let them humbly pray for me, a sinner. When they have received the longed-for devotion and blissful union, when they are consoled and refreshed, may they deign to remember my poor soul.

Chapter 18: The Importance of Faith

The Voice of Christ

Beware of vain examination of the Sacrament if you do not wish to be plunged into doubt. He who scrutinizes its majesty will be overwhelmed by its glory.

God can do more than man can understand. A pious and humble search for truth He will allow, a search that is ready to learn and to walk in the reasonable doctrine of the fathers.

Blessed is the simplicity that leaves the way of argument and goes forward on the firm path of God's commandments. Many have lost fervor because they wished to search into things beyond them. Faith is required of you, and a sincere life, not a lofty intellect or a vain investigation of mystery. If you neither know or understand things beneath you, how can you comprehend what is above you? Submit yourself to God and humble reason to faith, and the light of understanding will be given you. Some are tempted concerning faith and the Sacrament, but this is not held to them but to the enemy.

Do not be disturbed or argue in your mind. Do not answer doubts sent by the devil, but believe the words of God.

Believe His saints and prophets and the enemy will flee from you. It is often profitable for the servant of God to suffer such things. Satan does not tempt unbelievers and sinners whom he already holds securely. He tempts and troubles the faithful servant.

Go forward with unflinching faith, and with humble reverence approach this Sacrament. Whatever you cannot understand commit to the security of God Who will not deceive you. The man who trusts in himself is deceived. God walks with sincere men, reveals Himself to humble men, enlightens the pure, and hides His grace from the proud.

Human reason is weak and can be deceived. True faith cannot be deceived. Reason and natural science may benefit from following faith, rather than proceeding before or in opposition. In this holy Sacrament, faith and love are supreme and work in a mysterious manner.

God, eternal, incomprehensible and infinitely powerful, does great and inscrutable things in heaven and on earth. One cannot discern all His marvelous works. If the works of God were such that human reason could grasp them, they would not be beyond the power of words to tell or called wonderful.

AFTERWORD

In a normal and not unusual recent week there has been news of legal, moral and ethical violations committed by a variety of government entities, businesses and individuals. Almost always it was possible to trace these violations to the self interest of an organization or individual. Almost always there was an absence of humility, an absence of consideration for another. Actions reflected a spectrum of aggressive and sometimes predatory practices. Those affected often included the vulnerable (the ill or elderly, less educated or poor, the disadvantaged). Acts committed often required the participation of numerous decision makers as well as numerous implementers.

How does one who is a follower of Christ conduct themselves in such circumstances and matters? Often we may look down or away, not think about or understand fully the implications and aspects of what we do. We may try to merely focus on our immediate responsibilities. We do not think about or do not address the multiple effects of certain policies and acts within which we may participate. Such concerns have been relevant for me as an employee of businesses in a competitive marketplace. Such concerns have been relevant for my life within my local community and church. Those affected by legal, moral and ethical violations and actions are often my own friends and family, and the families and individuals I know in my town or church.

There can be a commonality and banality of ethical compromise and corruption. There is often a stepwise slide as no one individual or group faces an issue squarely or makes a decision with acknowledged responsibility. Decisions are disconnected from individuals and from identifiable parts of institutions. A business or government agency may seem to be impersonal. It may seem as if there is no place where decisions are clearly made or where responsibility rests. There is at times a pretense that matters do not have moral or ethical aspects or consequences. How do we apply the lessons and spirit of the *Imitation of Christ* to such matters? How do we go even further and face our responsibilities as individuals and organizations fully and clearly? How do we live our lives subject to a sincere and powerful faith in Christ? How can we be transformed by grace and faith and love?

Capitalism and democracy function more appropriately when they exist with markets and societies that are truly fair and transparent--which are conditions which must be enabled and worked toward. Our society has historically benefited from certain critical values and ethics, and from a belief that it is appropriate to pursue an overarching vision and purpose of establishing justice and mercy within our nation. For Christians there may also need to be submission to the sovereignty of God the Father, an indwelling of the Holy Spirit, and a constant imitation of our Lord Jesus Christ.

Sharing & Reviews

If this book has been helpful or a blessing, please share it with friends, and members of your family and community.

I would also greatly appreciate your review of this book at appropriate sites. Please use the title name *The Imitation of Christ with Devotional & Study Guide*. Please use both relevant author names: Thomas a Kempis and J. D. Nelson. Thank you for your time and consideration.

29039700R00085

Printed in Great Britain
by Amazon